T0196465

Teach a Child to Read

Written by Joyce M. Romanski
Illustrated by Brianna J. Miller

iUniverse®

TEACH A CHILD TO READ

Interior Graphics/Art Credit: Brianna J. Miller

iUniverse books may be ordered through booksellers or by contacting:

iUniverse
1663 Liberty Drive
Bloomington, IN 47403
www.iuniverse.com
1-800-Authors (1-800-288-4677)

ISBN: 978-1-5320-1748-3 (sc)
ISBN: 978-1-5320-1749-0 (e)

Library of Congress Control Number: 2017902122

Print information available on the last page.

iUniverse rev. date: 05/16/2017

I dedicate this book
to my mother, father, brother and friends.

Teach A Child to Read
A Guide for Teachers and Parents

Written by Joyce M. Romanski
Illustrated by Brianna J. Miller

About the Author

Joyce M. Romanski earned a B.S. degree from Marylhurst University with a major in elementary education. She earned a M.S. degree from Michigan State University in education with an emphasis on reading instruction. Joyce taught for 33 years in elementary schools, chiefly in the primary grades and in various reading instruction programs. She also taught reading instruction and testing at Portland State University.

About the Artist

Brianna J. Miller attended the Pacific Northwest College of Art and earned a B.F.A. in communication design. She was a PNCA Dean's Scholarship recipient and on the Dean's List all throughout her education. During her thesis year, she developed an interest in color theory and experiential design.

Contents

Contents

Part One: Strategies

Part One: Strategies

For the love of a story, learn to read!

Some students learn to read because of us. Others learn to read in spite of us. The purpose of this book is to give some handles to the student who needs assistance getting launched in the act of reading.

The tempo usually starts slowly and then picks up as the student gains skills and confidence. Show that you value reading and writing by getting caught in the act of doing these activities. Enjoy reading new and old favorite children's books with your student daily.

Increase your student's vocabulary by "talking up" to him/her. Try to use specific vocabulary. Be sure it is age appropriate.

Some General Comments for Decoding

1. Learn which lowercase letters the student knows. **Use the enclosed page.** Start with the lowercase letters. Most of the words that the student decodes are written in lowercase letters. The student should give the name of the letter, name of a picture that starts with that letter and the first sound of the picture. (Work on short vowel sounds first.)

   A suggested list of pictures for the letters has been included.

2. Learn the "Alphabet Song." Have student point to each letter as you sing it together. Learn a portion of the alphabet. Then add on a few more letters until the entire alphabet is mastered. (You can do both capital and lowercase letters at the same time.)

3. Master a small group of unknown letters at a time. Make multiple copies of each letter. Do about five letters at a time. After they are mastered, bundle them and set aside for review. Start with lowercase letters.

   (See specific steps at #5.) Go back frequently to review. Work on the capital letters after the lower case letters have been learned.

4. Make an alphabet book. Make one page for each letter. Write the capital and lowercase letter at the top along with a clue picture having the first sound of the letter. See enclosed page for clue pictures. Work on hard "c" as in cat and hard "g" as in goat. Add pictures to each page. (Work on short vowels in this book. Might want to leave blank pages for the long vowels to do later.)

Some Specific Steps

5. Present the cards individually. Student tells the name of the letter, gives the picture and then gives the first sound of the picture. Remember that the sound should be short and only give the first sound! Student keeps the cards that he/she responded to correctly; and teacher keeps the ones that need to be mastered. Make it gameful. It reduces stress! (Can do this in a small group situation.)

6. Move to telling name, saying pictures in head and then saying first sound. (Can do this while doing the activity stated in step 4.)

7. Finally, move to having the student name the letter and picture in head and then give the first sound orally.

8. Learn high frequency words as sight words or phonetically. On a large poster board, print these high frequency words multiple times randomly. Circle the phonetic words. Underline the word "I" and the letter "r" in the word "are"; say those letter names to say those two words.

Dictate sentences leaving out the high frequency words. Say "blank" for the missing words. The student gives the missing word each time and locates each one on the poster board. (Do a few words at a time.)

HIGH FREQUENCY WORDS/SIGHT WORDS

Names	Places	Actions/Feelings	Colors	Numbers
girl	house	see	red	one
boy	grass	like	yellow	two
man	sky	want	blue	three
woman	ground	went	purple	four
child	yard	do	black	five
children	school	does	brown	six
lady	street	go	orange	seven
people	building	goes	pink	eight
animal	church	run	green	nine
bird	library	ran		ten
dog	park	jump		
cat		walk		
pup		play		
kitty		ride		
grandmother		rode		
grandfather		stand		
bike		look		
horse				
ball				

You can add other words to these lists when they become frequent in the readings. Also make these words in the plural. Eventually, make cards with the words starting with a capital letter.

Sizes	Directions	Question Starters	Fillers	
little	up	Who	a	was
big	down	where	an	are
small	by	when	and	could
large	in	What	am	would
huge	next	How	for	should
tiny	then	Why	because	
round	inside			

Create a deck of picture cards. Students don't need to know how to read their spellings yet. However, print the word on the back for future use. Also make some punctuation mark cards.

Using tagboard, make a pocket chart to put on the bulletin board or on an easel. Give students portions of the deck of sight words and pictures. Dictate a short sentence to them. Have students contribute correct words/ cards to pocket chart to write the sentence. Remember to make some punctuation cards (. ! ?).

Be sure to put in spacing (two fingers worth) between words and end sentence with the correct punctuation mark. Remember to ask some question sentences. Continue doing this until the pocket chart is filled, and the group has a story. Try to start each sentence with a different word for interest and variety. (Point that feature out to the students so that they will pick up on that idea for their own writings.) Then have individual students read the story that they just completed composing (with teacher direction). Have the student read with pointing finger (the one that sits on top of the pencil). This is a way to check on word recognition and left to right direction. Collect the cards by asking the student to take off all the dictated words, such as "is." Continue until all the pockets are empty. Then create another story together in this procedure.

9. Eventually, move on to working on base words with endings (suffixes). Make a chart like the following:

jump	jumps	jumping	jumped
want	wants	wanting	wanted
like	likes	liking	liked
run	runs	running	ran

(Watch for change of vowel)

sing	sings	singing	sang
make	makes	making	made
fix	fixes	fixing	fixed
bake	bakes	baking	baked
ride	rides	riding	rode
sit	sits	sitting	sat

Add additional words to this chart as they appear in students' readings.

10. Short vowels always seem to need more attention. Learn them in a gameful way. Put a picture under each vowel on your "classroom" wall chart. Each picture should start with the sound of its vowel. For example, "a" is for apple, "e" is for egg, "i" is for igloo, "o" is for octopus and "u" is for umbrella. **The pictures should hint at the first sounds of the letters.**

   a. Give the sound. Then the student points to the correct vowel. Give the student several different vowel sounds. It is a quick activity for "filler times."

   b. Give the student the five vowel cards. Give a vowel sound. Then student shows the correct vowel that goes with each given sound.

   c. Also can do the procedures stated in 3, 4 and 5 above.

   d. Make lists of words using the short vowel sounds to read.

   At first, have the student read the lists down. Then have the student read the rows across. Watch to see if the student makes the change for the different vowels. **(Lists are provided in the book.)**

   Example:

pat	set	hit	not	hug
rat	ten	sit	hot	mug
mat	bet	bit	lot	rug
nap	wet	tin	dot	tug

   e. Compose a short story using mostly one of the short vowels along with some sight words. Make it into a booklet entitled, **The Short A Book.** Do the same for each of the vowels. You might want to make more than one booklet for one vowel sound. However, have one subject for each booklet. A short "a" booklet might be about a lamb. A short "e" booklet might be about an egg. The short "i" booklet might be about an igloo. Alternate between student and teacher supplying sentences for each booklet. This is a way to teach sentences and to check on observing punctuation marks. Be sure to compose stories with sentences ending in question marks and exclamation points too! **(Short vowel stories are provided in the book.)**

f.   Eventually, apply these games and activities to long vowel patterns. Make lists and write together short stories using the pattern that you are concentrating on mastering. **(See short vowel stories for ideas.)**

Examples:
    Pattern 1: at – ate, tap – tape, man – mane, hop – hope
    Pattern 2: ai as in tail
    Pattern 3: ay as in say
    Pattern 4: ee as in tree
    Pattern 5: ea as in team
    Pattern 6: ike as in like
    Pattern 7: ind as in find
    Pattern 8: as in ight
    Pattern 9: oa as in boat
    Pattern 10: old as in told
    Pattern 11: ow as in snow
    Pattern 12: y as in sky
        (List is provided in the book under long "i".)
    Pattern 13: y as in baby
        (List is provided in the book under long "e".)

11. Add compound words to master. (Provides a good introduction to syllables.) Put them on a chart or do in card fashion. Explain that each of the two parts of the word can stand alone. However, the dictionary says that they should be put together with no space between them. Make a pile of compound words. Cover the second words by folding them behind the first words. Have the student read the first part; then reveal the second part to continue making the compound word.

Here are some compound words to master. Choose a few at a time (six) to compose **short stories:**

into, someday, rainbow, greenhouse, cookbook, something, doghouse, bedroom, popcorn, everything, mushroom, grasshopper, everyone, housekeeper, lunchroom, today, lunchbox, breakfast, myself, wastebasket, pancakes, newspaper, outside, asleep, bedtime, homework, forget, tonight, someone, sunshine, grandmother, daytime, maybe, playthings, schoolbook, sunset, playhouse, notebook, storybook, fishnet, snowshoes, storybook, catfish, football, anyway, moonbeams, moonlight, everywhere, raincoat, truckload, birdhouse, tonight, blueberry, classmate, sailboat, dinnertime, sidewalk, toolbox, whatever, playground, fireplace, boathouse, suitcase, sawdust, snowshoe, beehive, fingertip, downhill, footstep, seacoast, birthday, birdhouse, doorstep, everybody, playpen, seafood, grownup, zookeeper, flagpole, butterfly, birdbath, homework, storekeeper, raincoat, shoelace, sandbox windmill, anyone, snowflakes, keyhole, indoors, firewood, weekend, waterproof, underline, sunroom, wallpaper

Add others as they appear in readings.

12. Using these strategies, apply to other reading/spelling combinations in the English language. See no. 4+.

   a. Consonant blends (two to three consonants before the vowel): br, cr, dr, fr, gr, pr, tr, bl, cl, fl, pl, sl, sp, st, sm, sn, sc, sk, sw, tw, str & spl
   (Lists are provided in book.)
   Write your own stories using these blends.

   b. Consonant digraphs: ch, sh, wh, th

   (Stories using these diagraphs are provided.)

   c. **Plurals: s & es (Note: −es follows s, x, ch and sh.)**

   d. Possessives

e. Contractions

f. Hard and soft "c" and "g" **(Lists are provided in book.)**

g. Vowel sounds controlled by "r" as in ar, er, ir, or and ur **(Lists are provided in book.)**

h. Diphthongs: oi, oy, ou, & ow **(Lists are provided in book.)**

i. Vowel "a" followed by "w" or "u" as in paw automobile

j. Long and short "oo" as in look and spoon

k. Silent letters as in knife, wren, gnaw, night, often and thumb

l. Prefixes and suffixes as in preheat, spoonful, unnecessary, redo, mismatch and midair

m. Synonyms, antonyms and homonyms

Here are some homonyms:

ate–eight	bear–bare	dear–deer	fir–fur	flea–flee
flour–flower	grown–groan	hair–hare	haul–hall	know–no
heal–heel	here–hear	hole–whole	knew–new	peace–piece
made–maid	new–knew	not–knot	pain–pane	some–sum
pear–pair	red–read	so–sew	steal–steel	to–two–too
sun–son	sail–sale	tail–tale	tide–tied	through–threw
waist–waste	way–weigh	week–weak	wait–weight	

Informal Survey on Knowledge of Letter Names and Letter Sounds

Write "Y" for yes and "N" for no under each letter after response. Do lowercase letters first, then do uppercase letters. Be sure to indicate if student gave long or short vowel sounds.

	Lower Case						Upper Case			
	m	d	f	g	a		D	F	M	A
Name										
Sound										
	b	i	t	o	s		T	S	I	B
Name										
Sound										
	k	j	p	n	c		J	K	P	C
Name										
Sound										
	h	l	r	v	y		R	Y	L	H
Name										
Sound										
	z	w	u	q	e		X	U	Q	E
Name										
Sound										
		x						W		
Name										
Sound										

Here are some suggested pictures to go with the letters. Learn letters' names, pictures and the first sounds of the pictures. The first sounds of the pictures should hint at the sounds of the letters.

A a is for apple.

B b is for bat and ball.

C c is for cat.

D d is for drum and stick.

E e is for Eskimo.

F f is for fish.

G g is for goat.

H h is for house.

I i is for igloo.

J j is for jar.

K k is for kite.

L l is for lamp.

M m is for mittens.

N n is for nail and hammer.

O o is for octopus.

P p is for pig.

Q q is for queen.

R r is for rat.

S s is for snake.

T t is for table.

U u is for umbrella.

V v is for valentine.

W w is for web.

X x is for x-ray.

Y y is for yarn.

Z z is for zebra.

Writing and spelling are good ways to reinforce the skills.

A favorite way to begin is by retelling in great detail a not familiar fairytale or folk tale from a less familiar region or country.

1. Read the story to the student.

2. Before reading a second time, ask the student to listen for the important words that are necessary to retell the story. (This is good for developing vocabulary.)

3. Together make a list of the dozen most important words in the story.

   (Caution the student not to supply filler words: in, the, an, from, by, etc.)

4. Have the student retell the story from start to finish giving all the details.

   (This is good for sequencing, recalling details and building vocabulary.)

5. Pose a couple of questions to illicit missing parts. (This is helpful for recall of details.)

6. Pose some questions on what different characters' feelings might have been at certain times in the plot. (Elicit feelings.)

7. Ask the student how he/she might have felt at certain times in the plot. (Elicit feelings.)

8. Ask the student how he/she might have solved a problem in the story. (Calls for creative thinking.)

9. Ask the student to predict what might happen after the conclusion of the book. (Calls for plausible predicting.)

10. Plan an opportunity for the student to retell the story to an audience, even if it is only to another person.

11. Then have the student write the story using the important words. Model this activity by doing it first for the student. Show how to indent at the beginning of the story. Show how to stop at appropriate places for a breath indicated by a period. Might require that the student place one question sentence and one exclamation sentence in the story with appropriate punctuation. (Add this activity later.)

12. Eventually, you might want to have the student put in some conversations with quotation marks. (Do not attempt split quotations!)

13. Have the student read his retelling of the story aloud to you and someone else. Make this another public speaking opportunity.

14. Then move on to another less familiar tale and do the above steps. These activities are a comfortable way to get the student launched into writing his/her own stories. For his/her own story, have the student list his/her characters, locations, events and times before writing. Talk together and write down some possible first interesting sentences that would "hook" the audience. (Try to get the student off of starting with "Once upon a time..." and "This story is about...".)

15. Occasionally, you might want to start with the idea given in the first sentence of a trade book. Then have the student retell the story as he/she thinks it should have happened.

16. Another writing activity is to have the student interview a family member about an interesting experience from his/her past. (Provides an opportunity to be a reporter.)

17. Learning about the history of a monument/building/bridge in his/her city would be another interesting activity. Then writing it in one's own words would be a good writing experience. (Provides an opportunity to be an historian.)

18. Study the biography of a master artist. Write a short story of his/her life (about six sentences). Write one sentence at the top of each page. Have your student illustrate the sentence in the style of the artist.

19. Learn and retell the life of a famous explorer or discoverer.

20. Describe a painting, the exterior of one's house and the exterior of one's school.

21. Give directions on how to make something, such as mashed potatoes, a vegetable garden and setting the table. Require that each sentence begin with a different first word: Firstly, Then, Next, After and Finally. May repeat first word once but not in the following sentence.

22. Make a book of familiar phrases that your family uses around the house.

23. Make a book of favorite recipes from family and friends.

24. Make a book of lists: favorite colors, favorite sports, favorite songs, favorite books, favorite movies. Could be students' favorite things, or family members' favorite things or friends' favorite things.

25. Use the significant vocabulary of a story to make a crossword puzzle.

Here are some groups of words to master gradually through the writing process:

Group 1	Group 2	Group 3	Group 4
one	for	man	right
once	four	many	write
to	ate	end	people
too	eight	friend	purple
two	of	here	sun
you	off	hear	son
your	where	deer	quit
by	were	dear	quiet
buy	pray	red	quite
three	prey	read	though
there	tail	say	thought
their	tale	says	through
the	no	said	threw
they	know	so	pie
way	new	sew	piece
weigh	knew		
are	blue		
our	blew		
some			
sum			

Together write short definitions after each word.
These words appear frequently in students' writings.

Short Vowel Drills and Stories

A is for apple.   E is for egg.   I is for igloo.

O is for octopus.   U is for umbrella.

1. In the beginning, read these lists down.

2. Then read them across. Watch for change of vowels.

1. hat	net	mitt	pot	mug
2. map	pet	wig	not	hug
3. cat	send	bit	cot	nut
4. nap	wet	kit	dot	bug
5. rat	bet	sit	lot	cut
6. sat	beg	dig	top	tug
7. bat	leg	rip	mom	sun
8. dad	egg	fit	rot	sum
9. fat	hen	big	log	gum
10. ran	let	fin	dog	run
11. bag	mend	wig	not	lump
12. fan	pet	bit	fog	dug
13. rag	red	pit	jog	jug

3. Write short stories using words from one list at a time.

4. Eventually use words from all of the lists.

The next pages have examples of step 3.

One Lamb

One lamb is in the grass. I see a pan in the grass. What is in the pan? Is it sand? Is it jam? No! I see water. The lamb likes it. The lamb ran to it. The lamb looks at the water. The lamb wants it. The little lamb laps the water. It is so good!

Big Hen

Ted likes the pet. The pet is a hen. Do you see the hen? Ted sees his hen. I see the big hen too! The hen is wet. It is in a big pen. Yes, the hen likes his bed in the big pen. The eggs are in the hen's bed. The bed is a nest. The hen sits on the seven eggs. Will the eggs open? Not yet!

Big Pig

One big pig sits on a hill. Will the pig zip down the hill? Yes, he will! Will the pig give us milk? No, the pig will sit. Tim likes the pink pig. The pig will dig and dig. He will dig by the mill. Will this pig go for a swim? Yes, he will! Today is a good day for a swim!

My Dog

My dog likes to trot. Do you see him hop? No! My dog likes to trot a lot. He will not go by a cop and a mop. He trots in the fog. See my dog trot! He does not run. Yes, he trots in the fog. Do you have a dog? Does your dog like to trot?

The Duck

The duck runs and runs. I see him run in the dust. He runs in the mud and dust. I will have to put him in a tub. My duck will not jump out! He will have fun and go back in the sun when I am done. See him back in the sun? Yes, I see him in the sun. My duck likes the sun.

Some Long Vowel Drills and Stories

1. not – note   tap – tape   cap – cape   man – mane

2. tap – tape   fad – fade   rat – rate   Ned – need

3. ten – team   bed – bead   met – meet   hop – hope

4. ran – rain   fed – feed   fin – fine   Sid – side

5. mill – mile   ran – rain   bat – bait   Tim – time

6. rod – rode – road   Sal – sale – sail

7. rid – ride   hug – huge   cot – coat   bat – bait

8. can – cane   pin – pine   rod – rode   mad – made

9. tub – tube   hat – hate   kit – kite   plan – plane

10. rid – ride   at – ate   us – use   pan – pane

Long *A* Vowel Patterns

a____e	a____i	-ay
cane	tail	say
make	wait	may
game	pail	day
rake	rain	pay
same	sail	ray
tame	paint	lay
cake	main	hay
mane	pain	bay
came	mail	stay
date	jail	way
name	fail	sway
fade	hail	today
ate	nail	play
wade	quail	clay
bake	rail	*they*
lame	bait	
sale		

24

A Long *A* Story

May and Ray want to play a game. They like to play the same game. They came to my house to play the game.

Mother made a cake for us. After our game, we ate some cake. Mother put our names by the plates. We ate our own cake!

Then Ray and May went home. They had to walk in the rain. Then hail came! So they ran! They ran fast to their own home. They can't wait to come again.

Long *E* Vowel Patterns

ee	ea	ea	-y
free	eat	heat	baby
tree	bead	seal	happy
see	leap	tea	jolly
keep	lean	read	windy
three	deal	seal	sunny
bee	meal	each	rainy
seem	leave	beach	pony
feed	team	reach	lucky
need	heal		hobby
seed	beam		nearly
weed	clean		funny
queen	dream		sorry
deep	beat		beauty
heel	peal		
feet	real		
feel	bean		
beet	seat		

Long Vowel *E* Story

The Queen has some free time. She wants to plant some seeds. She has three seeds. So she will dig three holes. She wants to put one seed in each hole. So she does. Then she sits under a tree. She sees her plants in a dream. The plants need water. So she feeds them water.

Now the Queen needs a cup of tea. So the Queen leaves the seeds. She cleans up. Now she can have a cup of tea. She will have some cookies with her tea. The Queen looks at the sea while she eats. Next she will read or go to the beach!

Long *I* Vowel Patterns

i____e	i____e	___ind	-y	___ight
like	slide	find	try	night
ride	prize	mind	sky	sight
wipe	smile	wind	my	fight
ripe	file	kind	why	might
bike	hide		fly	light
fine	while		by	bright
mile	kite		dry	fright
dive	wise		fry	right
line	side			
five	bite			
wide	awhile			
time	nine			
white	fire			
pine				

Long Vowel *I* Story

Tim wants to go for a ride. He will take his white bike with him. He can go for one mile. It will take some time!

On his trip, he will ride by some trees and vines. He will ride in the bike lane. He will stay on the right side of the line. Also, he will stop at the light.

Tina wants to fly her kite. The idea puts a smile on her face. She will go by the side of her house. The wind was kind. It took the kite up as high as the pine tree. It stayed up for a while. It was always in her sight!

Long *O* Vowel Patterns

o_____e	oa	__old	ow
hope	boat	sold	mow
rope	coat	fold	slow
note	load	cold	snow
bone	road	told	flow
cone	toad	sold	bow
vote	toast	old	row
joke	moat	mold	show
pole	float	gold	blow
those	soap		

Long Vowel *O* Story

Joe has a cold. He wants to go to school. His cold is better. His nose is better. So he goes to school. He had a note from his dad. He had a joke to tell his class.

Will it snow? No, it was not cold enough! Mom made him put on his coat. It was cold on the road. He stood by the pole for his bus. His bones got cold. Then the bus showed up.

At school, Joe told his joke. The girls and boys liked it. They voted it as the best joke of the day.

Y As Vowel Story

It was a pretty morning. The sun was out! It was very sunny. It was a very sunny morning. We looked at the sky. We say birds fly by. It was very dry outside.

Then it got ugly. The rain came. It became a rainy morning. Why did it rain? The grass will like the rain, but the pony will not! Will the puppy like it?

Mother told us to come and hurry in. She wanted us to get dry. She was sorry about the lovely day. Maybe it will be lovely again!

Consonant Digraphs –sh, th, ch & wh

sh for shoe	th for thumb	ch for chin	wh for wheel
shell	thing	chick	whip
shut	thumb	chess	whisk
shot	thank	church	when
shop	them	champ	where
shrimp	thick	chest	what
ship	than	check	which
short	then	child	whiff
shelf	there	children	
brush			
crash	with	inch	
dash	tenth	pinch	
cash			
mash	width	branch	
hush		bunch	
ash		fetch	
flash		match	
cash		crutch	
rush		hatch	
		ranch	
		stitch	

"Sh" for Ships

Columbus came across the ocean on a small ship. Two other ships came across the same ocean with him. The ships came with the food and the water that they needed. It took these ships many days to cross the ocean. The men on these ships got tired. They wanted to go back to their homes. Columbus wanted these three ships to keep going west. So they kept going west.

One day they saw birds. That meant that they were near land. Yes, they finally saw land. They were happy. This meant that they could get off the ships for some days. On land, they might find some fresh food to eat.

After the long trip, did the ships need fixing? One of the ships really did need help. The men from the ships met the people who lived on this new land. The land really wasn't new to the people who lived there, but it was new to the men who came from ships. The men saw different plants and animals.

Draw a picture of the ships that they took across the ocean.

Draw a picture of a ship that they might take today.

"Sh" for Dishes

Mother and father put good food on our dishes. They worked hard to fix the food for our dinner dishes. They washed vegetables and fruit. They cooked the food in pots and pans on our stove. When the food was cooked just right, they put the food on our dishes for our dinner.

Our family has dishes with pretty designs on them. The dishes are round. Around the sides of the dishes are beautiful flowers. There are blue flowers, red flowers and yellow flowers. We are very careful with the beautiful dishes.

After dinner, the children wash these dishes for mother and father. Only the children who are old enough get to do this job. We want to take care of our beautiful dishes.

A company has asked you to design a pattern for a new dish. Make a picture of the design you would draw for that dish company.

"Th" for Thumbs

My fingers and thumbs go into my mittens. Now my fingers and thumbs will be warm. My mother made the mittens for me. She used needles and yarn to make them. I like them very much. When the snow comes, I put them on. My brother and I make snowballs. When the mittens get wet, we go inside. We hang the mittens to dry. Then we have some cookies and hot chocolate.

Draw a picture of a clothesline. Hang some mittens on the line.

"Th" for Path

The rabbit hopped down the path. The path went through a patch of flowers. The rabbit stayed on the path through the flowers. Then the path went through some grass. The rabbit hopped on the path through the grass. Then the path went through the forest. Sometimes the path went by short trees. Sometimes the path went by tall trees. The rabbit liked seeing all those trees.

It was dark in the forest, but the rabbit stayed on the path. He did not get lost because he stayed on the path. When he got to the end of the path, he was at home. His home was in the trunk of a thick tree. He was thrilled to be home. In fact, he was thankful to be home. This was the best place of all! His mother was glad to see him again. She did not thump him for being gone so long. She gave him a bath with soap and water. The soap and water took the filth off. Then she saw that her rabbit was thin. So she made him a delicious supper.

Does this story remind you of another famous story?

Draw a picture of the path with the things that the rabbit will see along the way.

"Ch" for Champ

Are you a champ at something? People who are champs are good at something. A champ may be good at doing something. Maybe the champ is good at making something, or maybe the champ is good at collecting something.

A champ can be good at doing something well. Maybe the champ is good at playing the guitar, playing basketball or playing chess. Are you good at doing something well? What is it? Tell us what you are good at doing!

Maybe the champ is good at making something. Maybe the champ is good at making cookies, making salads or making ice cubes. Are you good at making something well? What is it? Tell us what you are good at making!

Perhaps the champ is good at collecting something special. Maybe the champ collects stamps, collects coins or collects rocks. Are you good at collecting something? What is it? Tell us what you are good at collecting.

A champ might be good at doing all three things: doing, making and collecting. These activities become hobbies.

Make lists of doing, making and collecting activities.

"Ch" for Lunch

Our family is going on a picnic. That means that we take our very own lunch with us. Before we go we put things we need for our lunch in a basket. The food for our lunches goes in the cooler. For lunch, we want sandwiches, apples and milk. Also, mother thinks we might want water with our lunches too. Father thinks we might like some watermelon in the cooler. He puts it in the refrigerator the night before our picnic. Then it will be cool for our lunch. We like that idea a lot.

We usually have our picnic lunch in the country. It is a good idea. In the country, we see bunches of grass. We find a good place to sit for our lunch. At the end of lunch, father chops the watermelon open. Then we eat it with our knives and forks, or we can use our teeth for knives and forks. The dessert is so good. We are glad our mother and father take us on picnics for our lunches. It has to be a good day when we can see the sun – no clouds!

Draw pictures of the foods that will come out of your cooler for your picnic lunch.

"Wh" for Wheels

We see wheels all around us. Big wheels! Little wheels! Thin wheels! Fat wheels! Girls and boys like the wheels that make their bikes go round and round. Even mothers and fathers like good, strong wheels on their bikes.

Mothers and fathers are happy when the wheels on their cars are in good shape. Those thick, strong wheels help them get to work and to the store. Sometimes those cars with thick, strong tires get their children to school and to the public library. School buses have thick, strong tires also. Those wheels will help the buses get the children to school.

There are many trucks on the road with thick, strong wheels. We need those trucks. They bring clothes to stores. Those trucks bring helpers to our homes to fix things. Wheels even spin wool into yarn. Then we can knit our own clothes! What would we have to do if there were no wheels? We would have to walk! So we are thankful for those wheels!

Make a picture of your bike with its two wheels.
Make a picture of your family car with its four wheels.
Make a picture of a school bus with its thick, strong wheels.

Consonant Blends

Keep the sound going from one to the next to make the blend.

Add additional words to the lists as you find them.

br	cr	dr	fr	gr
bring	crib	drink	front	green
brown	creek	drop	frog	grass
brave	crack	draw	frost	gray
brush	cry	drum	from	ground
broom	crop	dress	free	grab
bridge	cross	dry	fruit	grew
bread	crown	drove	fresh	great

pr	tr	bl	cl	fl
print	trip	blue	class	fly
pretty	truck	black	clean	flag
president	train	blew	clay	flat
press	track	blood	cloud	flower
prize	tree	blanket	clock	floor
promise	trail	block	cloth	flew
present	trade	blow	close	flash

pl	sl	sp	st	sm
plan	slip	spoon	stick	smell
plate	slept	spot	star	small
play	sled	speed	still	smart
plant	sleep	spin	store	smoke
please	slow	spent	stand	smog
place	slid	space	step	smooth
plane	slick	spell	stop	smash

sn	sc	sk	sw	tw
snug	scoop	skill	swan	twin
snake	scold	skirt	swim	twist
snow	score	sky	sweep	twelve
snail	screen	skin	swing	twenty
sneeze	scoot	ski	sweet	twirl
sniff	school	skunk	swirl	twinkle
snap	scare	skid	swift	two

Soft "c"

cent   juice   circle   city   dance   fence   celery

face   mice   place   fancy   cement   center   ceiling

cider   fence   decide   circus   cinder   circumference

Hard "c"

cake   cat   cup   cage   candy   coat

catch   call   can   cross   cone   cute

came   cap   cold   cut   come   cry

Soft "g"

age   orange   magic   giant   page   hinge   ginger

gym   judge   badge   stage   germs   bridge   message

gerbil   juice   edge   general   ginger   germ   geology

Hard "g"

goat   game   gum   gate   glue   got

gorilla   go   good   garden   give   get

gold   gift   gave   gone   get   goose

Vowel Sounds Controlled by "r"

–ar	–er	–ir	–or	–ur
far	her	fir	for	curl
jar	fern	girl	sort	burn
mark	person	first	corn	fur
yard	serve	dirt	north	hurt

Diphthongs – ou, ow, oi, & oy

ou	ow	oi	oy
mouse	cow	coin	toy
south	how	soil	boy
town	town	boil	joy
count	tower	foil	loyal
mouth	crown	joint	Roy
round	down	point	soy
found	now	oil	

Mastery of these beginning decoding skills should launch your student into the act of reading.

Comprehension
Kinds of questions:

1. Literal: noting details

    Example: Name some of the things that Marie suggested that Rosa and she should do to make Rosa forget about the thunderstorm.

2. Literal: cause-effect

    Example: Why was it hard for Rosa to concentrate on her activity?

3. Interpretive: drawing conclusions

    Example: How did father help the girls even though father was at work?

4. Interpretive: making inferences

    Example: If Marie had been home alone, why would she have been afraid of the thunderstorm?

5. Evaluative: thinking critically

    Example: What might have happened if Marie had been as scared of the storm as Rosa?

6. Interpretive: drawing conclusions

    Example: How did having the radio turned up loudly help Rosa forget about the storm?

7. Evaluative: relating reading to experience

    Example: In a thunderstorm which of the girls would you have acted like?

8. Interpretive: making inferences

    Example: What made Marie the courageous babysitter?

While reading a new storybook or chapter book, stop occasionally to ask the students to make predictions as to what will happen next.

Print a piece of poetry on a large piece of paper. Cover a couple of key words. Ask the students to give other words that might fit in those spots.

Give students the middle of a story. Ask them to dictate or write their beginnings and their endings of the story.

Give the students an ending of a story. Ask them to dictate or write their beginnings and middles of the story.

Part Two: Reader

A is for airplane pilot.

One boy sees the plane.

One girl sees the plane.

It is in the sky.

See the plane go.

The sky is blue.

See the plane in the sky.

It is in the blue sky.

Do you see the plane fly?

The boy sees a plane.

It is up in the sky.

The girl sees it too.

Do you see it?

Yes, I do.

The plane is big.

Very big!

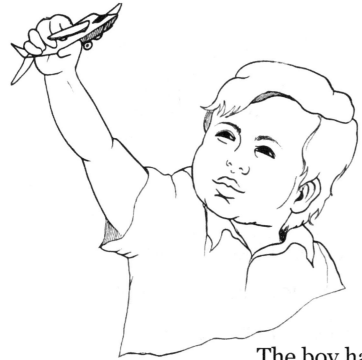

The boy has a plane.

It is little.

Do you see it?

It is in his hand.

The little plane has two colors.

His plane is red and green.

Can it fly?

The girl likes the big plane.

The boy likes the big plane.

They want to go on it.

They want to go on a trip.

It has two big wheels.

Does the little plane have wheels?

Yes! Where are they?

Mom sees the plane.

It is going up, up and up.

She likes it.

The plane is up in the blue sky.

It is high.

It is high in the blue sky.

See it go!

Dad sees the big plane.

Dad wants to go on a plane.

Mom wants to go on

the big plane.

They want to go on a trip.

All of us want to go.

We will go on the plane.

B is for baker.

Do you see a baker?

The girl and boy

see the baker.

He likes to bake.

He likes to make cakes.

He makes big cakes.

Mmm! They will be good!

The girl likes cake.

The boy likes cake.

They want some cake.

Do they see the big cake?

Yes, they see the cake.

The baker made a big cake.

It is very big!

The baker has pots.

The baker has pans.

Pots and pans help.

They want to help him bake.

He likes to make cakes.

He makes lots of cakes.

Girls like big cakes. Mmm!

Boys like big cakes. Mmm!

Girls like big and little cakes. Mmm!

Boys like big and little cakes. Mmm!

They look at the cake!

It looks good!

Do you see the cake?

It is a big cake.

Do you see the little cherries?

Yes, we see the cherries.

Do you see the six candles?

Yes, we see six candles.

One girl wants cake.

One boy wants cake.

Who made the cake?

The baker made the cake.

He likes to make cakes.

Do you like to make cakes?

Yes, we do.

We make cakes at home.

C is for cowboy.

We see a horse.

The horse is tall.

Do you see the tall horse?

It is very tall!

A cowboy is on the horse.

How did he get up there?

One boy sees the horse.

The horse is very tall.

One girl sees the horse.

It is very tall!

The girl likes the horse.

The boy likes the horse.

It is a very tall horse.

A cowboy is on the horse.

He likes the horse.

He wants to ride the horse.

Where will he go?

Will he go to the grass?

Yes, he will.

The girl wants to pet the horse.

The boy wants to pet the horse.

Will they pet it?

Yes, they will. See them pet it?

Do you want to pet the horse?

Yes, I do!

The cowboy has a big hat.

It is big. It is black.

The boy has a hat.

It is little. It is black.

Does the girl have a hat?

No, she does not have a hat.

See the man go!

He is going to the grass.

The grass is green.

It is very green!

The horse likes grass.

He likes green grass.

See the horse go!

D is for doctor.

I see the doctor.

The doctor sees me.

I tell the doctor that

I feel good.

I am getting tall.

I eat good food.

Look at me! I am tall!

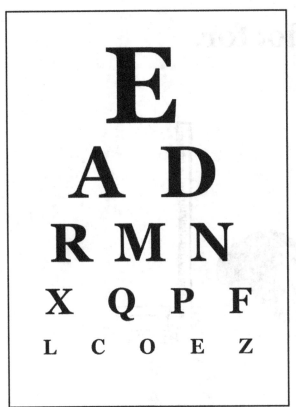

The doctor looks at my two eyes.

My eyes are blue.

They are big and blue.

Look at them!

The doctor wants me to look at the E.

I can see the E and ADRMNXQP.

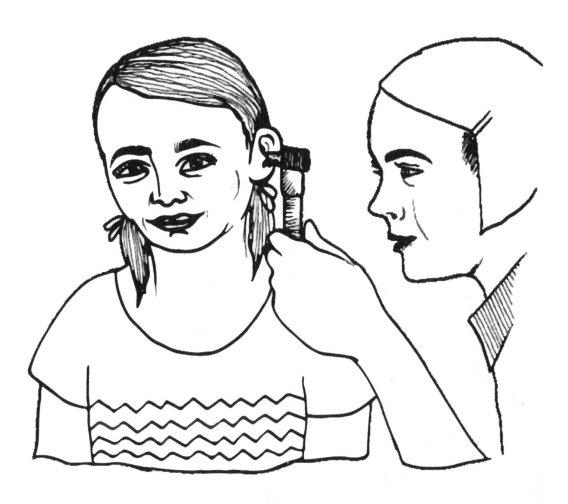

Then the doctor looks at my ears.

I have two ears.

I hear with my two ears.

The doctor tells me that I hear well.

I am happy about that.

I love to hear music!

I can find AB and C.

I look at DE and F.

I can do my ABC's.

The doctor hears me say them.

Look at me do them!

They will help me in school.

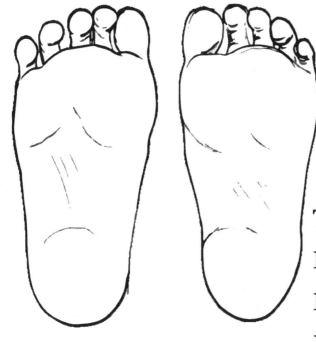

The doctor looks at my feet.

I have two feet.

I can run fast with them.

I can jump with them.

I can swim with them.

I love to run and jump!

My doctor is tall.

My doctor helps me.

He looks at me.

He likes what he sees.

I am strong. I feel good.

I can run, jump and swim.

E is for engineer.

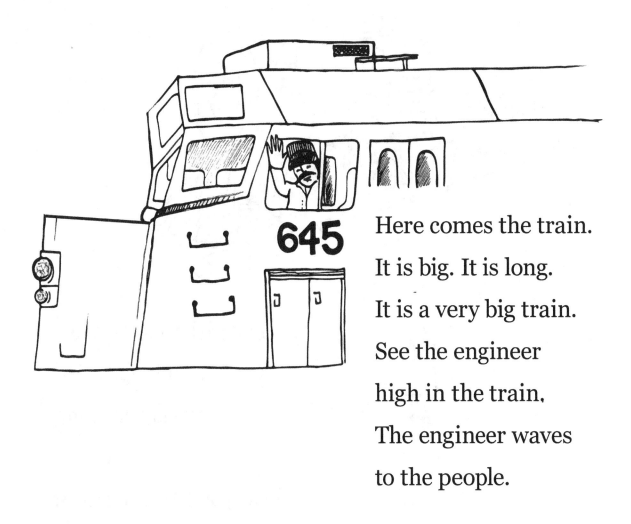

Here comes the train.
It is big. It is long.
It is a very big train.
See the engineer
high in the train,
The engineer waves
to the people.

The girl sees the train.

She sees a long train.

The train is very long.

It is red and black.

Do you like the train?

Yes, I like the train.

The girl likes the train.

She likes it a lot.

Do you see the engineer?

He is up high.

See him up high.

The engineer makes the train "toot."

The train goes "toot, toot, toot!"

The train goes down the track.

The engineer stops the train. The train stops at the end of the track. The girl gets to see the train better. She likes the colors on the train. The train is red and black. Are all trains the same colors?

The girl wants to go on a train.

She wants to take a ride on the train.

She wants to go on a trip.

Her mom and dad will take her on

a trip. It will be a very long trip!

They will go to see friends!

Do you want to go on a trip?

Yes, I want to go on a train.

My family wants to go on a train.

We want to go on the train to California. Some day we will take a trip on the train.

F is for farmer.

Where is the boy?

Today he is on a farm.

See the cows? He sees three cows.

He will go up to one of the cows.

Does the cow see him?

One cow sees him.

The brown cow sees him.

It is fun to go to a farm.

Milk comes from cows.

Cows give good milk to people.

The boy likes milk.

It is good for his bones.

We must have milk.

"Mmm! Good!"

Do you see a black cow?

Yes, I see one black cow.

She has four legs.

She eats grass. She gets good food.

Do you see a red cow?

No, I do not see a red cow. Do you?

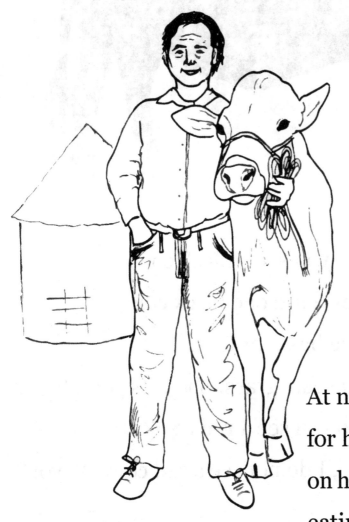

At night, the farmer looks for his cows. The cows are on his farm. They have been eating grass. The cows walk around the farm. They look for grass. They find lots of grass on the farm.

The farmer takes the cows home.

He shows the cows to the barn.

The cows walk to the door of the barn.

They go into the barn, one by one.

Each cow goes to its own place.

The cows stay inside for the night.

The barn is very big.

The farmer likes his big barn.

It is big and red.

People see the red barn from far away.

The barn has a second story for hay.

The farmer gives the hay to the cows.

My family likes to visit
a farm. The farmer asks
us to come. We love to
see the cows and the barn.
When it is hot, the cows
are under the trees. They
sit under the trees. It is
cool under the trees.
Do you see them?

G is for grocer.

See the good food.

Some food is round.

Some food is long.

Some food is red.

The grocer sells some

yellow bananas.

They are long and yellow.

At home she ate the yellow
bananas. Now she must go
to the store again. Mother
and she will walk to the store.
See her walk with her mother.
Her mother and girl walk fast.
They go to the store again.

The grocer has apples
and carrots too. Mother
must get some good apples.
She will buy the apples from
the grocer. Also she needs
some oranges. She buys three
oranges. The little girl asks
mother to buy some bananas.
Mother does. She thanks the
grocer for them.

A farmer brings the food to the grocer.

He brings fresh fruit and vegetables.

The grocer wants us to eat good food.

The farmer brings the food in his truck.

He comes everyday with good food.

Do you see the farmer's truck?

It has fresh fruits and vegetables.

The grocer has other fruits and
vegetables. See the other foods.
In summer, he sells strawberries and
blueberries. People like these berries.
In fall, he sells squash and pears.
Other people come to see the grocer.
They want to buy good food too!
They take the fresh food home to eat.

People want buy to lettuce and
tomatoes for their salads.
People want to bake potatoes for dinner.
Mothers want to give their children
some strawberries to eat.
Which fruits do you like best?
Which vegetables do you like best?

H is for house builder.

The builder has one hammer.

He has one saw for the job.

Do you see the hammer?

Yes, I see it with the man.

He hits the nails with the hammer.

Do you see the saw? Saws cut wood.

No, I do not see the saw with the man.

The man has the hammer.

The man is up high.

He must be up high.

He is on a ladder.

He has one hammer

and three nails.

He hammers the

three nails. This

will help the house.

Look at the house!

It is pretty.

Do you like it?

It is a good house.

It is strong.

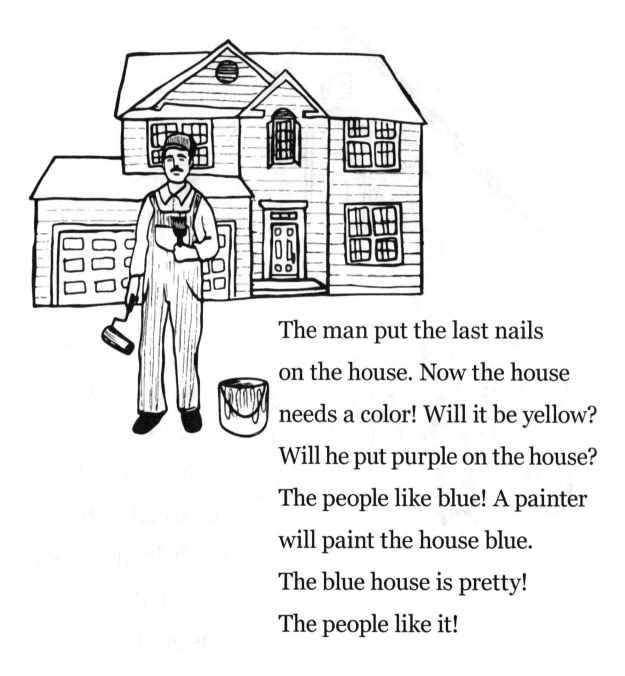

The man put the last nails
on the house. Now the house
needs a color! Will it be yellow?
Will he put purple on the house?
The people like blue! A painter
will paint the house blue.
The blue house is pretty!
The people like it!

Other people want homes of their own.

They want the builder to make homes

for them. The builder makes them.

One family wants a tall house.

They want a home with many windows.

The windows will let in lots of light.

The family wants it painted green.

Another family wants a home in the country by some horses. They want the builder to build a long home. The builder will do it. They are happy about the news. There will be many trees near it. Trees will keep the family cool in their home. They like trees.

The builder goes to
a lumber store. At
the lumber store,
he gets wood to make
the house. He buys a lot
of wood. The builder
buys wood from fir trees.
Fir trees give us strong
wood to make houses.
The builder buys nails too!

I is for ice cream maker.

At this store people make ice cream.

Girls and boys like ice cream cones.

This girl and boy will get two ice cream

cones. They love ice cream!

Do you love it too? It is good!

How much does one cone cost?

One ice cream cone costs one dollar.

This ice cream maker makes the best

ice cream in town!

Mother likes ice cream too!

She likes to lick it too!

The girl and boy saw her eat brown ice cream. It was chocolate ice cream.

She likes chocolate ice cream.

They know she does.

Mother always buys that kind.

The boy likes pink ice cream.

It is strawberry ice cream.

The girl knows he likes this kind.

She saw him lick it.

It looked good! "Mmm...good!"

He ate all of it.

The ice cream was cold.

It was very cold!

The girl likes ice cream too!

She stops to get ice cream.

She stops at the ice cream store.

A woman sells her some ice cream.

It was very good. "Mmm! Good!"

The girl takes the ice cream from

the store. It was good and cold!

Other people stop at this store.

Some people buy vanilla ice cream.

Some people buy chocolate ice cream.

Children buy peppermint ice cream.

Dogs watched them lick their cones.

Cats watched them lick their cones.

Some people buy tubs of ice cream. They take the tubs of ice cream home. Their families will have ice cream later. Some people make ice cream at home. They have machines to do the work. Today the machines use electricity. Long ago people made ice cream by hand.

J is for judge.

One woman sits up high.

One man stands before her.

They hear each other talk.

The man tells his story to the judge.

He tells everything that he knows.

He wants the judge to know everything.

This judge asks many questions.

The man gives his answers.

They work hard to know the truth.

Both want to do their best.

The judge knows the rules.

He wants to help the man live

by the rules. The man knows this.

They have a lot of work to do.

The judge and the man work for many hours.

They go from 8 a.m. to 5 p.m.

Then they go home on the bus.

They need time to think and rest.

The next day they will meet in the

judge's room.

The woman told the judge about her dog.

Her dog was on a leash.

The neighbor saw the dog running freely.

The judge said that by law the

dog needed to be on a leash.

The woman knew that law.

She told the judge that her dog ran off.

This judge called for the neighbor.

The neighbor stood before the judge.

The judge asked the neighbor questions.

The neighbor didn't see the leash on the dog.

The judge told the woman the law

again. Then the judge sent them home.

K is for kennel owner.

This woman takes care of dogs.

She takes care of cats too.

She likes dogs and cats.

She likes to make them pretty.

She cuts the dog's hair.

Now the dog looks better.

She cuts, combs and pets my dog.

The vet will give the dog a drink.

The dog likes water.

The dog must have some water.

He drank the water.

Where is the water?

It is in a cup, a big cup!

The water felt good. "Mmm! Good!"

Will some cats come today?

Yes, some will come.

Cats like milk.

Will they get some milk here?

Yes, they will.

The cats will drink the milk

because they like it.

"Mmm! Good!"

Milk is good for them.

Some dogs are well.

They feel very good.

Some dogs are sick.

They feel ill.

The vet will look at

the sick dogs.

My dog is very well

today. See him smile!

My dog feels good.

He feels very good.

My dog runs. My dog jumps.

My dog swims too!

See him run! See him jump!

See him swim!

He does a very good job

swimming!

I love to play with my dog!

Some dogs and cats are big.
Some dogs and cats are little.
Some dogs are still puppies.
Some cats are still kittens.
Both like to run and jump!
They like to play. Do they
play with each other?
Sometimes they do!

L is for librarian.

This woman likes books.

She takes good care of books.

She gives the girl a red book.

The girl wants to read the red book.

Boys like books too!

The red book is a good book with

lots of words and beautiful pictures.

This room has many books.

Do you like books?

Some books are big.

Some books are little.

The girl will read some books.

It is fun for her. She is happy!

Many people like books. Some books make people laugh. Do you like to read funny books? The red book makes the girl laugh. She knows how to read it. The librarian helps the girl find books. Librarians know what children like!

Books tell us how to do things.

Books tell us how to make things.

Books tell us how to collect things.

Which kind of books do you like?

Do you have a hobby? Perhaps you

will find a book about your hobby.

Do you dance, make kites or find

beautiful rocks? Find books on them.

People love to go to the library.
They look for books on the world
  about birds and about planets.
Some love to look at beautiful
pictures. Others look at maps.
The librarian helps them find books.

Some people have little libraries at home.
Some libraries are little. Others are big
with books on hobbies. Cooks have
cookbooks in the kitchen. Bike fans
have some magazines on bicycles.
Knitters have books on patterns.
Do you have books on your hobby?

M is for mail carrier.

Here comes the mail carrier.

She has a big bag at her side.

The bag is full of letters and magazines.

She takes the bag from house to house.

She walks from street to street.

She puts letters and magazines in boxes.

People are happy to see the mail carrier. They hope he brings them letters from friends and neighbors. Perhaps! Sometimes they get magazines about the news or their hobbies. Sometimes they receive letters about their water, their telephone and their electricity.

Sometimes the mail carrier goes to stores. He brings letters, magazines and packages to the owner of the store. Sometimes he takes letters to the fire department. Sometimes he takes letters to the police department. These people hope to receive good news!

Trucks carry letters and packages
from city to city. These trucks are
very big. The trucks take letters
and packages to the post offices.
Big cities have big post office
buildings. Little cities have little
post office buildings. The letters
are taken inside these buildings.
People sort the letters and packages.

We buy stamps for our letters and packages. Stamps come in different sizes and prices. It takes less money to buy a stamp for a letter. It costs more money for a package. The money pays for the mail carrier, the trucks and the post office buildings. Do you collect stamps for a hobby?

Some letters need to go far away.

Some packages go far away too.

It costs more to send them far away.

Some letters and packages go to
a far away country. Have you ever
sent a letter to far away place?
Airplanes and boats take them away.

N is for nurse.

I see one nurse.

This nurse helps the little girl.

The little girl wants help.

She is glad to have help.

Now she feels better.

She is happy!

The little girl is happy now!
She feels good now. Now she
can run and play with the other
children. She is glad about this.
It is fun to run and play. Other
sick girls and boys go to the
nurse for help.

The nurse lets the girl look around
her office. Her office has things to
help girls and boys when they feel
sick. The office is very clean.
The nurse makes sure it is clean
every day. It must be clean. Germs
can make people sick. People do not
want to be ill. It is no fun to be ill.

The nurse went to school for many years. She learned how to take care of sick people. She learned how to help them feel better. Then the nurse took tests to see if she knew what to do. This nurse knows what to do. Girls and boys are glad that she is there for them!

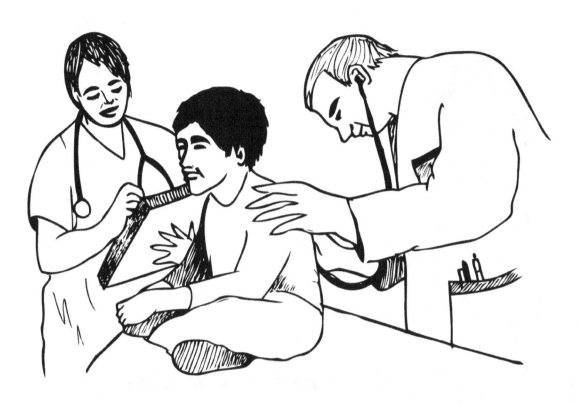

Is your mother a nurse?

Is your father a nurse?

Maybe they are doctors.

We need people like nurses

and doctors to help people.

They are teachers too! They

teach us to eat good foods,

get fresh air and exercise.

Do you?

Some nurses work in schools.
Some nurses work in offices.
Some nurses work in hospitals.
Have you ever been to a doctor's
office? Have you ever been to a
hospital? Maybe you visited
someone in the hospital!
Hospitals help many people
get well!

O is for office staff.

See the lady on the phone?
She works here. What does she
do here? I think I know! She helps
people. She just knows how. In fact
she went to school to learn about
her job. She was a good student.
This is good news! She helps people
with their questions. This is good
news! Yes, it is!

I want to ask the office staff a
question. I will wait my turn.

When Mrs. Smith gets off the phone,
I could talk to her. Mrs. Smith
works in this office.

The staff works here on Monday,
Tuesday, Wednesday, Thursday
and Friday. The staff is here all week!
Their weekend is free!

"Mrs. Smith, please help me!" She looked at me with her round eyes. "I will try," she said. "Mrs. Smith, I lost my green mittens. Have you seen them?" She answered, "Yes, I have. Here they are! When you get home, be sure to write your name inside each one."

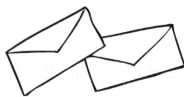

The office staff knows how to spell. They write letters on their computers. They even have dictionaries and telephone directories in their desks. The news goes out by e-mail or by letter. Also in their desks, they have stamps to put on the letters. Moms, dads, teachers and students are glad to get this mail.

The office staff looks at their calendar every day. They learn what activities are happening in the building each day. The office staff makes sure that boys and girls get to the right places every day! They help mothers, fathers and guests find the right rooms.

The office staff checks to see if the
building has the needed supplies.
Does the building have enough
pencils, paper and envelopes? The
office staff orders the supplies
for the building. Teachers tell
the office staff what they need.

P is for police officer.

I see a big police officer. He wants to help me. I need to cross the street. The police officer helps me get across the street. He stops the cars and trucks for me. He used his whistle. It was loud. He made the street safe for me!

Every day the police officer sees many cars, trucks, bikes and walkers. Some cars are big. Some cars are little. Some trucks are big, and some trucks are little. The police officer always looks out for us. He does his best! He wants to help us.

I see a big yellow truck.

The police officer sees the same yellow

truck. This truck needs to stop!

The police officer blows his whistle

two times. He puts his hand out

to tell the truck to stop! See the

truck stop. We see the truck stop for us.

The police officer helps other boys and girls to cross the busy streets. We must always stop to look and listen. The police officer tells us to stop and listen many times. Then we can cross the street. See the girls and boys walk across the street now! All people need the police officer's help!

I will go to school. I like school.
Some girls and boys ride the school
bus to school. Some mothers and
fathers drive their children to school.
I walk to school. The police officer
helps me get there carefully. At school
I can do my work. I like my work!

To be a police officer, a man or woman has to study the rules and laws. She or he has to go to a special school to learn how to be a good police officer for the city. Police officers exercise and eat good food to be fit for their work. Also they have to know how to get along with people.

Q is for quarterback.

I like to play football. When I grow up I want to be a quarterback too. I want to be just like him. He is tall and very strong. He works hard. He eats good food, exercises and gets enough sleep! I must try to do those things too. I must grow strong even if I do another job in life.

A quarterback runs fast. First he catches the ball. Then he runs and runs with the ball. He doesn't want to drop the ball. He runs away from the other team. His team tries to help him. The team wants a touchdown. That would be great! The quarterback works hard!

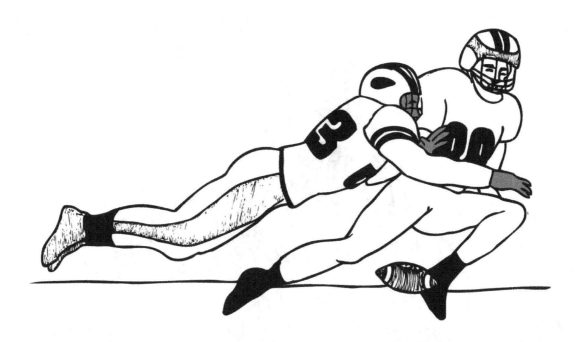

Sometimes the quarterback falls.
Then he picks himself up with
the ball in hand. Again he runs
and runs. He wants to get to the
goal to make a touchdown. He
will work hard to do that. He
likes to run. With his strong
legs, he will run very fast, just
like the wind!

If his team wins, the players will be very happy! They will carry him up high. The team likes to win! Yes, they do. The fans like that too! Sometimes the team loses. When the team loses a game, the players smile and walk away nicely. The players are very good sports!

There are many sports to play. You could play tennis, soccer, softball and volleyball. Do you have a favorite sport that you love to play? Girls and boys love to play their favorite sports with their families and friends. They especially like to do it on sunny days!

You can do some sports outside. Some sports are done inside. One inside and outside sport is swimming. People go to neighborhood pools to swim. They might do a few laps or play safe games in the pool. They follow the pool rules. Guards help them do this.

R is for rocket builder.

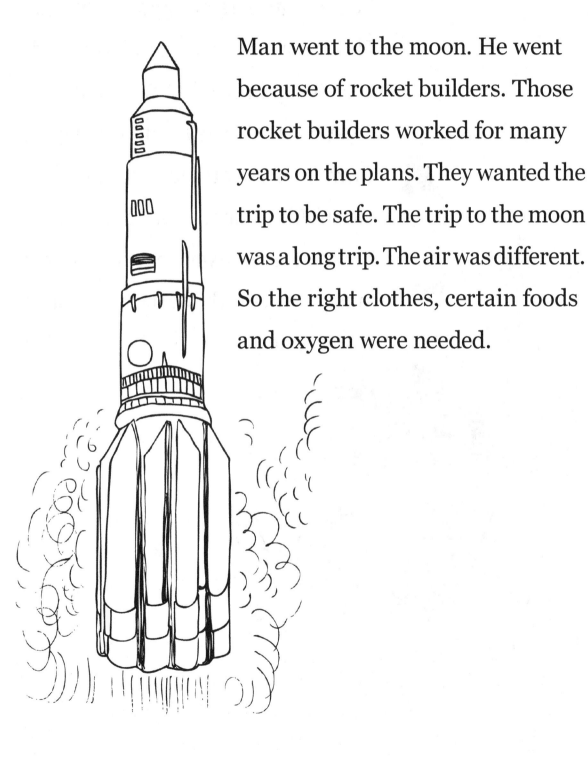

Man went to the moon. He went because of rocket builders. Those rocket builders worked for many years on the plans. They wanted the trip to be safe. The trip to the moon was a long trip. The air was different. So the right clothes, certain foods and oxygen were needed.

Rocket builders are good at math. They work on their plans over and over. They know that their plans must be right. They want the trips to go well. Man wanted to go to the moon. Man must be able to come back to Earth. Every part of the plan must work. So they study the plans many times.

The rocket builders wanted someone to go who likes to fly. The astronaut must know how to read well. He must be good at math. He wouldn't be able to stop on the way to the moon for help. Once he lands on the moon, he could get out. He is able to walk around for a short time. What did he find? Surprises?

On the moon an astronaut will see rocks, dust and craters. A crater is a cup-shaped dent in the moon's crust. Scientists think craters were made when meteorites, comets and asteroids hit the moon. Some craters were filled by lava. Many astronauts have walked on the moon.

Would you like to
help build a rocket?
It takes many workers
to build a rocket. They
have to read plans and
do lots of math. They have
to work together. Many
people work on the plans
for the rocket. Would you
like to go to the moon?
Why would you like to
go there?

There are other planets. Venus and Mars are near us. Can life live on those other planets? Scientists are trying to learn the answers. Do other planets have water and plants? Are their lands smooth or rocky? Maybe both! These planets are far, far away. Do we have rockets that can go far?

S is for singer.

Singers love to sing! They want to sing. Singers sing songs. Can we sing those songs? Perhaps! Some singers sing high notes. Some singers sing low notes. Most singers work to sound better. They want the notes to be pretty! They love beautiful music. Beautiful music sounds good to us!

Singers like to listen to music on the radio. They pick their favorite place on the radio. Maybe their favorite singer will sing on the radio. Maybe! Perhaps they will hear their favorite songs. Do you like to sing? Do you have a favorite song? Do you have a favorite singer?

Sometimes we buy music sung by our favorite singer or band. When we have music, we can listen to it in our free time. Sometimes our mothers and fathers like the same singers. Our mothers and fathers might like the same songs. Do you sing with your mother or father? Sometimes!

Where do you find your music? Do you watch for sales in the paper or online? Maybe your favorite music is on your birthday wish list! Perhaps you work to get the money. When you get enough money, you can buy your favorite music. It will be fun to listen to your favorite music!

Some singers sing by themselves. They play the piano or strum a guitar while they sing. Singers might sing slowly, or they might sing fast. Do you like to listen to fast or slow music? Does your favorite singer like fast or slow songs? Maybe the singers sing both speeds.

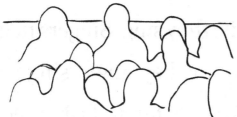

Some singers sing with an orchestra. Other singers sing with a band. There are some singers who sing with an orchestra one night and a band the next night. They like both kinds of groups. Do you like to hear your singer with a band or an orchestra?

T is for teacher.

Many people are teachers. Mothers and fathers teach their children. Nurses teach girls and boys how to take care of themselves. Dentists teach people of all ages how to take care of their teeth. Have you ever helped someone learn how to do something?

School teachers work very hard. They try to listen to each child every day. They plan to help all the children to read and to do math. Every day teachers read the papers that the girls and boys finished. Teachers love to see their students grow in so many ways!

Teachers love to read too!
Every day they read a book
to their children. Often they
read an old favorite book to
the class. Sometimes they
read a new book to them.
It is good to hear a new
book. Teachers also do math.
They do it fast!

This teacher wants to help.
All teachers want to help.
Now this teacher walks
around the room to help.
When girls and boys like
to read, the teacher is very
happy! These children like
to read. See how happy they
are! They love books! They
love to read every day. They
read at school and at home.

Teachers are real people too. They buy food for their meals. They wash their dishes. They grow flowers and run with their dogs. Also they love to read a good book before they go to sleep. Yes, they stop to floss and brush their teeth!

Often teachers are students too. They go back to school to learn some new ideas. Other teachers show them some new ideas in math and reading. They also take classes in science. Just like the children, they learn about some new artists. Then they show their new ideas to the children.

U is for United States President.

The people are waving good-bye. The man with the papers has a new job. He is the president of the U.S.A.! The president is flying to Washington, D.C. He is going there to make good laws for all of us. It is difficult work. He wants to do the right thing for all of us.

Why is the man going to the White House? He won! The people voted for him. The people think he can do good work for them. This man will help write laws. Then he will help pass the laws. Our country needs good laws. The people in our state will tell him what they want!

What kind of laws do we need?
We need laws on air, water and taxes.
People write letters to our capital in
Washington, D.C. Sometimes the people
send e-mail letters. The people tell their
ideas. Everyone wants the best for our
country. What are your ideas?

The president is leader of our army, navy, air force and coast guard. He needs to be sure our country is safe. He checks these groups to see if they are strong. Do these groups have the equipment they need? Do they have good doctors, nurses and hospitals? The president checks to see what is needed.

The president talks to leaders in our country. He listens and talks to mayors, governors, senators and the vice-president. He wants to help schools, police, fire fighters, bridge builders, and road makers. He finds money to help these different needs. People pay taxes to help. They say, "I need to pay Uncle Sam!"

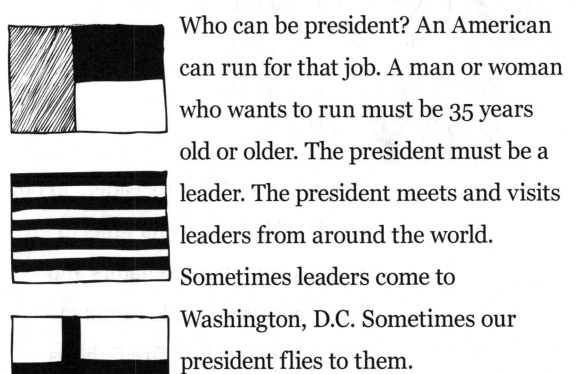

Who can be president? An American can run for that job. A man or woman who wants to run must be 35 years old or older. The president must be a leader. The president meets and visits leaders from around the world. Sometimes leaders come to Washington, D.C. Sometimes our president flies to them.

V is for violinist.

The violinist is playing her violin. She looks at the music. The music has notes on it. The notes tell her what to play. She hopes to play beautiful music. She doesn't play alone. Two men play with her. Together they play a song. You might know it.

Some days the violinist plays with many other people. Some might play the violin. Some might play the drums. Some might play the flute. They play their favorite instruments. They love to make music together. Together they make a beautiful sound. We love to listen to their song. Sometimes we go to a concert to hear our favorite group play.

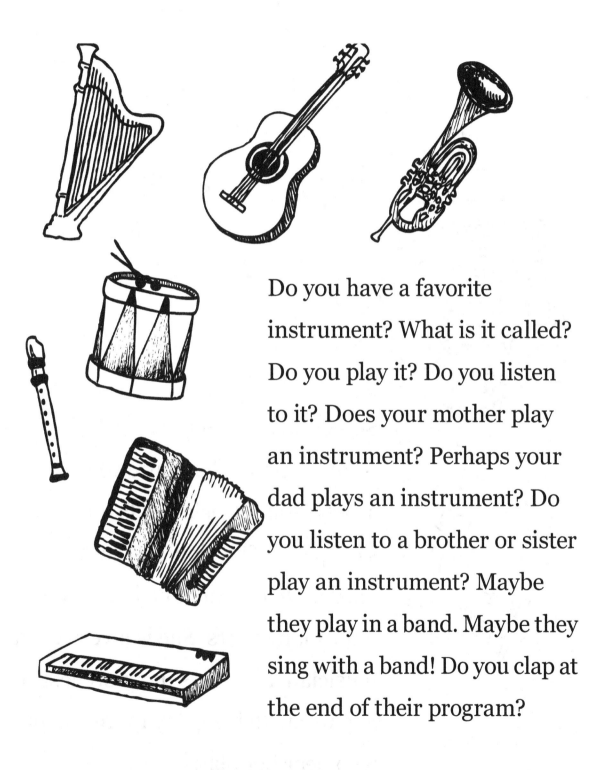

Do you have a favorite instrument? What is it called? Do you play it? Do you listen to it? Does your mother play an instrument? Perhaps your dad plays an instrument? Do you listen to a brother or sister play an instrument? Maybe they play in a band. Maybe they sing with a band! Do you clap at the end of their program?

Sometimes the music goes fast. At other times the music goes slowly. Some music has fast and slow parts. The violinist works hard on her violin. She has played it for many years. She is a very good musician. She plays in an orchestra. She wants to bring joy to the people who hear her play.

Different instruments are made
with different materials. Some
are made out of wood. Others are
made from brass. Some
instruments have ivory on them.
Other instruments have reeds
on them. The player might
use his fingers, or the player
might use sticks to beat the
drum. Other players might
blow on their instruments
to make the sounds.

You might find some unusual instruments in different places. In Australia, you might find the didgeridoo. In Hawaii, you might hear more ukuleles. In Russia, you might listen to the balalaika. Where will you hear the bongo drums? Where is the marimba popular?

W is for weather reporter.

The weather reporter tells us what is coming. He might tell us that it will rain. We are used to that in our city. He might tell us that it will be sunny. Maybe the day will be sunny at first and rainy later. After we hear the news, we will know what clothes to use. Maybe we will need an umbrella and boots.

The weather reporter wants to help us. He wants us to wear the right clothes each day. He wants us to walk with care. He wants our mothers, fathers and bus drivers to go with care. The weather reporter studies weather maps and weather instruments to help us. He does his best! Do you study your thermometer?

Is today a good day to go swimming? It doesn't look like it. When it is sunny again, the children will go to the park. They love to play in the park on sunny days. Will the rain clouds fly away? The girls and boys hope so!

An umbrella is good for rainy times.

Boots are good for rainy days.

Sunglasses are good for sunny days.

Caps are good for sunny day days.

A shovel is good for a snowy day.

Snow tires are good for snowy days.

May ice stay away. Far away, every

day! What kind of weather

do you like?

The farmer needs the right weather to grow her crops. She needs the sun to help the seeds get started. She needs the rain to give the plants the water to drink. Even the wind helps take seeds to a good home to grow. However, if the farmer's crop gets too much sun or too much water or too much wind, her plants might not become healthy plants. Good weather is needed.

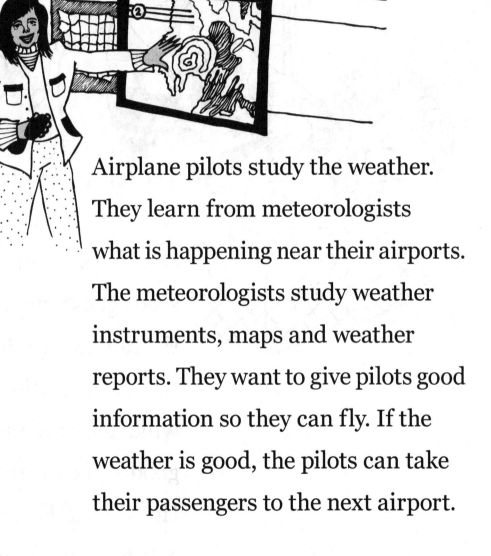

Airplane pilots study the weather. They learn from meteorologists what is happening near their airports. The meteorologists study weather instruments, maps and weather reports. They want to give pilots good information so they can fly. If the weather is good, the pilots can take their passengers to the next airport.

X is for x-ray person.

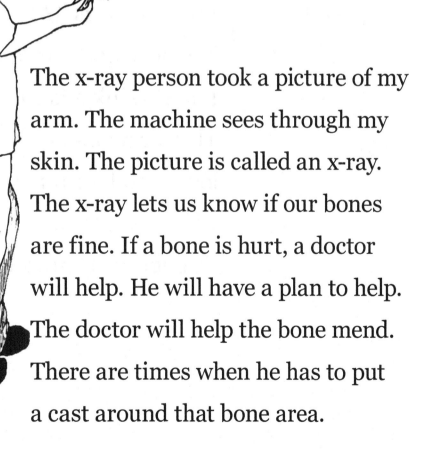

The x-ray person took a picture of my arm. The machine sees through my skin. The picture is called an x-ray. The x-ray lets us know if our bones are fine. If a bone is hurt, a doctor will help. He will have a plan to help. The doctor will help the bone mend. There are times when he has to put a cast around that bone area.

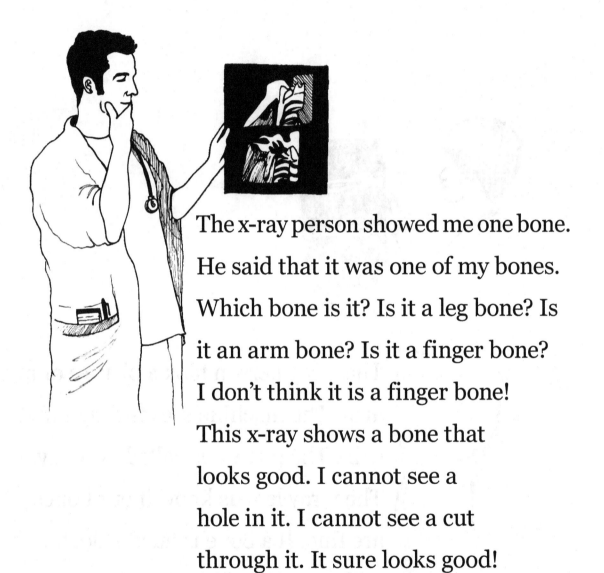

The x-ray person showed me one bone.

He said that it was one of my bones.

Which bone is it? Is it a leg bone? Is

it an arm bone? Is it a finger bone?

I don't think it is a finger bone!

This x-ray shows a bone that

looks good. I cannot see a

hole in it. I cannot see a cut

through it. It sure looks good!

When I ride my bike, I watch where I go. I stop at the right places. It is important to take care of my bones. I am not going to hurt them. I drink milk to make strong bones. Mother says that I am doing a good job! My dad is pleased about my good habits.

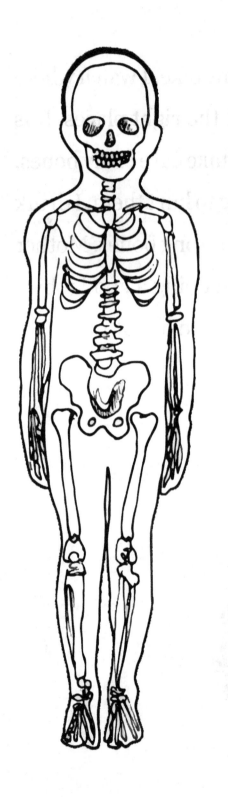

Bones hold the body up. We need bones. They help us to stand and walk. All of our bones together make our skeleton. We need our bones. We want to run, skip and jump! So we need our bones. They hold us up! They help us to move and they protect the other soft parts inside of us! Also parts of bones help make our blood.

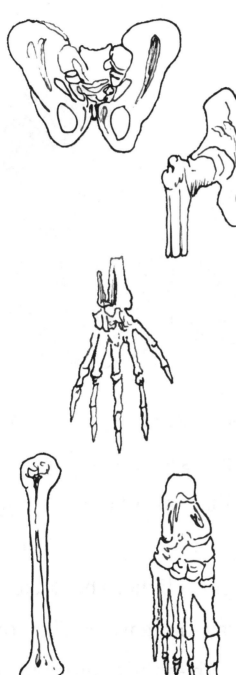

Some bones are long.
Some bones are short.
Some bones are thick.
Some bones are thin.
Bones are hard. There
are 206 bones that go
together to make a
person's skeleton. Look at
the bones in meat and fish.

When we are born we are only a
few inches long. Our bones
grow like our other body parts,
until we are all grown. Sometimes
we break a bone. The doctor takes
an x-ray to see where the bone
broke. Then the doctor puts on a
cast to put the broken bone together.
Another x-ray will tell the doctor
when the bone is mended.

Y is for yarn maker.

In a book I see a woman at a spinning wheel. What is she doing? She is turning the wheel. It is important to make the wheel go round and round. See the woman push the pedal? The pedal goes up and down. This pedal makes the wheel go round and round.

Some wheels are large. Some
wheels are small. All the wheels
can turn the wool into yarn.
When the wheel turns it puts
twist in the wool. The twist
makes the wool turn into yarn.
The woman spins the wheel
many times each day. It is her
job. She needs to make many
inches of yarn. Yarn keeps us warm!

Where does the yarn maker get the
wool? Sheep give us wool. In spring
the farmer cuts it off the sheep.
This helps the sheep to cool off.
The yarn maker buys bags of cut
wool. She takes the bags of wool
to her home. Then she opens the
bags to admire the fleece. After
that, she washes all of the
wool. "Good-bye, dirt!"

What does the yarn maker do with the new yarn? She might keep the yarn in its first color. Or she might turn the yarn into different colors: green, blue, yellow or purple. After that she might sell some of the yarn. With the yarn she keeps, she will knit into warm clothes. She might knit socks, mittens and sweaters.

There are many people who need warm clothes. So many people need to spin wool into yarn. In fact people have built factories to do this work. Big, fast machines do fast spinning. The machines give us yards and yards of yarn. These yarns come in natural colors and dyed colors. Have you seen these yarns at the store?

Did you know that other animals give us their coats to make yarn? Which animals do that? Llamas and alpacas are two popular animals that also give us beautiful, soft yarn. Do you know the kind of yarn that made your sweater? Look on the label.

Z is for zoo keeper.

The zoo keeper helps to take care of the animals. The zoo keeper has many animals at the zoo. Most of the animals are in very big cages. The zoo keeper wants to give the animals good homes. So they make their homes look like the real ones.

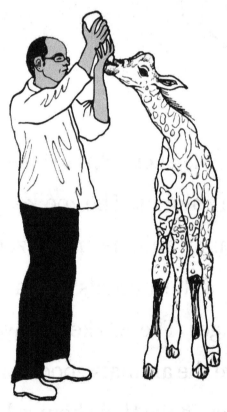

Some of the baby animals need extra help. So they put these animals in the zoo nursery. The zoo keeper gives them the extra food, extra pats and warm beds that they need. Sometimes people can see the baby animals through the glass windows. Look for the special babies at the zoo.

The zoo keeper makes sure the animals eat right. She plans the right food for each of the animals. Some animals eat vegetables. Some animals like fruit. Some animals eat meat. The zoo kitchen fixes the food for the animals. The helpers take the food to the cages.

The animals come from different places in the world. The animals are different sizes. Some animals fly. Other animals swim. You will see tall animals and short ones. Which ones do you like to watch? Do you watch the lions, elephants, bears, giraffes, camels and monkeys?

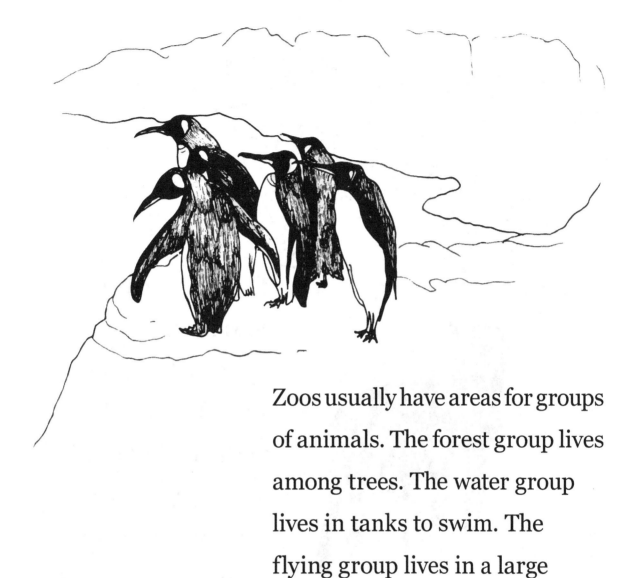

Zoos usually have areas for groups of animals. The forest group lives among trees. The water group lives in tanks to swim. The flying group lives in a large space to glide and land. Study the map that your zoo gives to learn where to go. You might have a favorite spot.

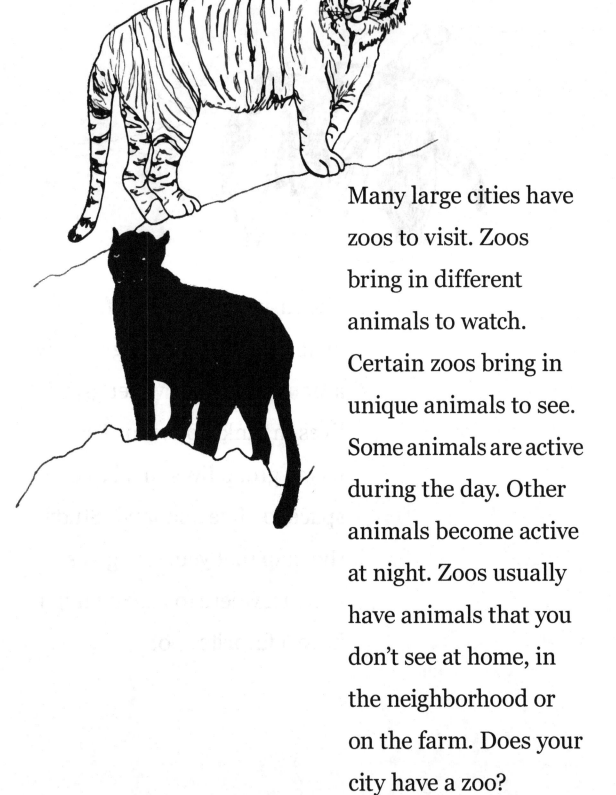

Many large cities have zoos to visit. Zoos bring in different animals to watch. Certain zoos bring in unique animals to see. Some animals are active during the day. Other animals become active at night. Zoos usually have animals that you don't see at home, in the neighborhood or on the farm. Does your city have a zoo?

Part Three: Bibliography

Reinforcement Activities:

A bibliography of trade books to go with each job has been attached. Even if your student isn't at the point of decoding these books, he/she can learn the concepts and vocabulary (by ear then by sight) on these subjects as you read them.

Here are some activities to do with each story. Might want to do a different activity for each job. It's all right to repeat an activity for a different job. Repetition in the beginning reduces stress.

1. Start with this activity orally to teach the concept of answering question sentences with answer sentences. The emphasis is on learning the concept of a **sentence.** Ask a question about the story. The student answers by using a couple of words from the question sentence to start the answer sentence. Have students fold a large piece of blank paper in half to make a booklet. Have the student draw a line on the fold - front and back to keep the place. The front page is the title page. Have the students write **The Airplane Book** by (his/her name). Teacher writes question sentences (one for each page on a piece of paper or chalkboard). The student copies the three sentences (one at the top of each of the following pages). Then the student answers each sentence under each question sentence with proper punctuation. Under each sentence, the student illustrates the answer. The illustration should match the answer.

2. Together teacher and student make a list of words/names of things that that worker uses. Make a picture after each word.

3. Teacher writes a scrambled sentence about the worker being sure to use the vocabulary that the story uses. The student unscrambles the sentence starting with the capitalized word. Be sure to practice this activity on the chalkboard first. Practice by having individuals place numbers above the words to show the correct sequence. Then have individuals write each sentence in the correct order. Do this several times. Then give the student three scrambled sentences (one

per page) to do in his/her booklet like the one stated in **number 1.** Illustrate each sentence.

4. Create a deck of cards using the words and pictures in the story. Make multiple cards of the same words. Dictate one word at a time – to write – a new story in the pocket chart.

5. In a small group, the teacher uses her deck of cards on the story to see how many students in her reading group can correctly read and receive the cards. Teacher keeps the cards that they read incorrectly. At the end of the game, everyone counts his/her collection.

6. Write together a "spin-off" on one of the trade books about the job you are studying at the time. Teacher models the first story. Students supply some interesting (general in nature) first sentences for their own stories. Write them on the board. Each student selects the one he/she wants to start for his/her own story. Or he/she can still write another for his/her own opening.

7. Write a direction booklet "accordion style" about the job. Try to start each sentence differently, using starter words like first, then, after, next, etc. Student might think of some other starter words.

8. Together, write a poem or song about the job.

9. If appropriate, design a new uniform for the worker. Write a description about the outfit.

10. If appropriate, create a new tool for the worker. Label the parts. Tell how the new tool works.

11. Draw a map of the worker's workplace. Label the places. (Be sure to teach aerial view in advance.)

12. Write safety rules for the worker's workplace.

13. Tell how the job was done in the past. (Bring in some trade books that would show the activity in previous years. Show the time on a simple timeline on a piece of paper or chalkboard.)

14. Tell how the job might be done in the future.

   For numbers 13, 14 and others, remember to model doing these writings before assigning the student to do these activities.

15. Have the student take a yellow crayon to highlight all the words he/she can read on a page in the newspaper. (Be sure to select appropriate pages or articles.) Inform him/her that this is what the older students do to locate important facts quickly!

16. Create a cartoon with frames and balloons for conversations between worker and customer. (This is an opportunity to stress manners for politeness and good customer service.)

17. Dramatize the above with stick figures drawn by the student and glued to sticks.

18. Tell what that worker needs to know in order to do his/her job.

19. Tell why you would like or not like to do that job when grown.

20. Interview a person (perhaps a parent) who does the job that the class is studying. Write "thank you" notes telling at least two new things that were learned. (Days before the arrival, gather questions to ask about the job.)

21. Go on a safe, permissible field trip to see the workers in action!

22. Make a list of other jobs that begin with that letter.

23. Eventually, the student might like to interview a parent about his/her work. Then have the student write about his/her work.

24. Start looking for local jobs. Learn about the different workers in the neighborhood and in the school building.

25. Reading, writing and storytelling

    a.) Reading additional fiction and fact books on a subject is reinforcing.

    b.) Writing the important facts (from informational books) is reinforcing.

    c.) Retelling a story in writing or in oral form is reinforcing.

    Do this activity before having the student do the following activity. After reading the book, together make a list of the dozen most important words in the book (not fillers words - in, the, of, from, for, etc.) Tell the student to be sure to use words in his/her retelling! A good book to launch this activity is *The Bremen-town Musicians* by Ruth Belov Gross and Jack Kent, published by Scholastic.

    d.) Check on comprehension with a variety of questions: tell main idea, recall details, note cause and effect, make inferences, make predictions, describe situations and characters.

Here are some books to enjoy together, even if the student is not at the decoding level of the selected book. The books are grouped according to concepts. Try to do one of the suggested activities with each of the books. Although some of the books are not in print, you might find them at the library, in book stores, at sidewalk sales and on the internet. Be sure to preview each book before presenting it. And be sure that each book is one that both of you would enjoy. Also be alert for other appropriate books to add to this list. New titles are arriving every day. You probably have favorite titles from your childhood that you would enjoy sharing. Keep reading to your student even after he/she has become a proficient reader. Books provide great opportunities for discussions.

ABC Books:
> *Dr. Seuss's ABC* by Dr. Seuss, published by Random House
> *ABC Potluck* by Anne Shelby, published by Orchard Books
> *Miss Spider's ABC* by David Kirk, published by Scholastic Press/ Callaway
> *Tomorrow's Alphabet* by George Shannon, published by Greenwillow Books
> *On Market Street* by Arnold Lobel, published by Greenwillow Books
> *G is for Goat* by Patricia Polacco, published by Puffin
> Wildflower ABC: An Alphabet of Potato Prints *by Diana Pomeroy, published by Harcourt Brace* and Company
> *Alison's Zinnia* by Anita Lobel, published by Greenwillow Prints
> *Alphabet Animals* by Charles Sullivan, published by Rizzoli
> *D is for Dancing Dragon* by Carol Crane, published by Sleeping Bear Press 310 N. Main Street, Suite 300; Chelsea, MI 48118
> *P is for Pilgrim: A Thanksgiving Alphabet* by Carol Crane, published by Sleeping Bear Press: 310 N. Main Street Suite 300: Chelsea, MI 48118
> *A Farmer's Alphabet* by Mary Azarian, published by Charlesbridge

Counting:
> *10 Little Rubber Ducks* by Eric Carle, published by HarperCollins
> *Rooster's Off to See the World* by Eric Carle, published by Aladdin Paperbacks

Waving: A Counting Book by Peter Sis, published by Greenwillow Books

Ten Terrible Dinosaurs by Paul Stickland, published by Dutton Children's Books

Ten Sleepy Sheep by Phyllis Root, published by Candlewick Press

1 is One by Tasha Tudor, published by Simon & Schuster Books for Young Readers

Ten Flashing Fireflies by Philemon Sturges, published by North–South Books

Counting in the Garden by Kim Parker, published by Orchard Books/Scholastic Inc.

1, 2, 3 to the Zoo by Eric Carle, published by Philomel Books

Moja Means One: Swahili Counting Book by Muriel Feelings, published by Puffin Books

Color:

Color, Color, Where Are You Color? by Mary Koski, published by Trellis Publishing Inc.

The Deep Blue Sea: A Book of Colors by Audrey Wood, published by The Blue Sky Press - An Imprint of Scholastic Inc.

Red are the Apples by Marc Harshman and Cheryl Ryan, published by Voyager Books/Harcourt Inc.

Red Leaf, Yellow Leaf by Lois Ehlert, published by Harcourt Inc.

Brown Bear, Brown Bear, What Do You See? by Bill Martin Jr., published by Henry Holt and Company

A Color of His Own by Leo Lionni, published by Dragonfly Books/ Alfred Knopf

My World of Color by Margaret Wise Brown, published by Hyperion Books

Patrick Paints a Picture by Saviour Pirotta, published by Frances Lincoln Children's Books

The Crayon Box that Talked by Shane DeRolf, published by Beginner Books/Random House

Language Patterns:

Does a Kangaroo Have a Mother, Too? by Eric Carle, published by HarperCollins

The Important Book by Margaret Wise Brown, published by HarperCollins

Have You Seen My Cat? by Eric Carle, published by Aladdin Paperbacks

Today is Monday by Eric Carle, published by Putnam & Grosset Group

Polar Bear, Polar Bear, What Do You Hear? by Bill Martin Jr., published by Henry Holt and Company

Brown Bear, Brown Bear, What Do You See? by Bill Martin Jr., published by Henry Holt and Company

I See the Moon and the Moon Sees Me by Jonathan London, published by Viking

Fireflies, Fireflies Light My Way by Jonathan London, published by Viking

Baby Bear, Baby Bear, What Do You See? by Bill Martin Jr., published by Henry Holt and Company

Shapes:

Color Zoo by Lois Ehlert, published by HarperCollins

Shape Capers by Cathryn Falwell, published by Greenwillow Books/ HarperCollins Publishers

Mouse Shapes by Ellen Stoll Walsh, published by Harcourt Inc.

Days, Months, Seasons and Time:

Today is Monday by Eric Carle, published by Paper Stars/The Putnam & Grosset Group

Chicken Soup with Rice by Maurice Sendak, published by Harper Row

Hickory Dickory Dock by Keith Baker, published by Harcourt Inc.

Monster Math School Time by Grace Maccarone, published by Scholastic

Grandmother Winter by Phyllis Root, published by Houghton Mifflin Company

A Book of Seasons by Alice and Martin Provensen, published by A Random House Pictureback

Summer by Alice Low, published by Beginner Books/Random House

White Snow Bright Snow by Alvin Tresselt, published by Lothrop, Lee & Shepard Co. Inc.

Seasons on the Farm by Jane Miller, published by Scholastic Inc.

Bring in the Pumpkins by Dahlov Ipear, published by Scholastic Inc.

Twelve Hats for Lena: A Book of Months by Karen Katz, published by K. Mcelderry Books/ Simon & Schuster

Groups:

Birds by Brian Wildsmith, published by Franklin Watts. Inc.

A Band of Coyotes by 4th Grade Students of Mabel-Canton Elementary in Mabel, Minnesota, published by Scholastic Inc.

Swimmy by Leo Lionni, published by Alfred A. Knopf

A Gaggle of Geese: The Collective Names of the Animal Kingdom by Philippa-Alys Browne, published by Atheneum Books for Young Readers

High Frequency Words:

Frog and Toad Are Friends by Arnold Lobel, published by HarperCollins

Little Bear by Else Holmelund Minarik, published by HarperCollins

Nate the Great by Marjorie Sharmat, published by A Yearling Book

Go, Dog. Go! by P. D. Eastman, published by HarperCollins

A Fish Out of Water by Helen Palmer, published by Beginner Books/ Random House Inc.

Ten Apples Up On Top! by Theo LeSieg, published by Beginner Books/Random House Inc.

I Read Signs by Tana Hoban, published by Scholastic Inc.

Mouse Soup by Arnold Lobel, published by Scholastic Inc.

Directions:

Up Above & Down Below by Sue Redding, published by Chronicle Books

All You Need for Snowman by Alice Schertle, published by Scholastic Inc.

How to Make Salsa by Jaime Lucero, published by Mondo

Poems:

Beast Feast by Douglas Florian, published by Voyager Books/ Harcourt Brace & Co.

Autumnblings by Douglas Florian, published by Greenwillow Books

Hand Rhymes collected by Marc Brown, published A Puffin Unicorn

Read-Along Rhymes for the Very Young selected by Jack Prelutsky, published by Alfred A. Knopf

Ladybug (the magazine for young children for ages two to six)

Spider (the magazine for children for ages six to nine)

Cricket Magazine Group: P.O. BOX 9304: La Salle, IL 61301-9897

Tortillitas Para Mama selected and translated by Griego, Bucks, Gilbert & Kimball, published by Henry Holt and Co.

Antarctic Antics by Judy Sierra, published by Gulliver Books/ Harcourt Brace & Company

Birthday Poems by Myra Cohn Livingston, published by Holiday House

Quotations:

Nibble Nibble by Margaret Wise Brown, published by Puffin Books

Barnyard Banter by Denise Fleming, published by Scholastic Inc.

Wake Up, Big Barn! by Suzanne Tanner Chitwood, published by Scholastic Inc.

Over in the Meadow by John Langstaff, published by Woyer Books/ Harcourt Brace & Co.

The Little Red Hen by Jerry Pinkney, published by Dial Books for Young Readers/ Penguin Young Readers Group

Barnyard Banter by Denise Fleming, published by Scholastic Inc.

Expressions:

Russell the Sheep by Rob Scotton, published by HarperCollins

Amelia Bedelia by Peggy Parish, published by HarperCollins

The King Who Rained by Fred Gwynne, published by Aladdin Paperbacks

A Chocolate Moose for Dinner by Fred Gwynne, published by Aladdin Paperbacks

Aerial View:

I Fly by Anne Rockwell, published by Crown Publishers, Inc.

The Great Zoo Hunt! by Pippa Unwin, published by Doubleday

Cross Section:

Stephen Biesty's Incredible Cross-Sections, published by Alfred A. Knopf

The Busy Body Book: A Kid's Guide to Fitness by Lizzy Rockwell, published by Crown Publishers

What's Inside? Small Animals by Angela Royston, published Dorling Kindersley/Scholastic Book Club Edition

History:

When Everybody Wore A Hat by William Steig, published by Joanna Cotler Books/An Imprint of Harper Collins publishers

Ox-Cart Man by Donald Hall, published by Scholastic Inc.

Potato: A Tale from the Great Depression by Kate Lied, published by National Geographic Society

When I Was Young in the Mountains by Cynthia Rylant, published by E.P. Dutton

Sam the Minuteman by Nathaniel Benchley, published by A Harper Trophy Book/Harper & Row

A Picture Book of Abraham Lincoln by David A. Adler, published by The Trumpet Club

A Picture Book of Martin Luther King Jr. by David A. Adler, published by Scholastic Inc.

General Store by Rachel Field, published by Scholastic Inc.

Homeplace by Anne Shelby, published by Orchard Books

Folk Tales, Fairy Tales, Myths and Traditions:

The Mitten adapted by Jan Brett, published by G.P. Putnam's Sons (Ukraine)

The Old Women and Her Pig (Ten other stories told by Anne Rockwell, published by Thomas Y. Crowell)

Anansi the Spider by Gerald McDermott, published by Henry Holt and Company

Juan Bobo Goes to Work: A Puerto Rican Folktale retold by Marisa Montes, published by HarperCollins

Aesop's Fables selected by Michael Hague, published by Holt, Rinehart & Winston

Lazy Jack: An English Folk Tale, published by Troll Associates

The Bremen Town Musicians by Hans Wilhelm, published by Scholastic Inc. (Germany)

Zomo the Rabbit: A Trickster Tale from West Africa told by Gerald McDermott, published by Harcourt Brace & Co.

The Three Wishes by Charles Perrault, published by Troll Associates (France)

The Brave Little Tailor by the Brothers Grimm, published by Troll Associates (Germany)

Snow White and Rose Red by the Brothers Grimm, published by Troll Associates

Peter and the North Wind retold by Freya Littledale, published by Scholastic Inc. (Norse tale)

The Legend of the Bluebonnet retold by Tomie dePaola, published by Scholastic Inc.

The Snow Child retold by Tomie dePaola, published by A Whitebird Book/ G. P. Putnam's Sons (Italian)

Whale in the Sky by Anne Siberell, published by E.P. Dutton (NW Native American)

Strega Nona retold by Tomie dePaola, published by Prentice-Hall Inc. (Italian)

Yoko's Paper Cranes by Rosemary Wells, published by Hyperion Books for Children (Japanese)

Throw Your Tooth on the Roof (Tooth Traditions from Around the World) by Selby B. Beeler, published by Houghton Mifflin Co.

Misoso: Once Upon a Time Tales from Africa retold by Verna Aardema, published by Scholastic Inc.

Reference:

Career Day by Anne Rockwell, published by HarperCollins

Days to Celebrate by Lee Bennett Hopkins, published by Greenwillow Books/HarperCollins

The Terrible Thing that Happened at Our House by Marge Blaine, published by Scholastic Inc.

Hand-print Animal Art by Carolyn Carreiro, published by Williamson Publishing

Picture Books to Enhance the Curriculum by Jeanne McLain Harms & Lucille J. Lettow, published by the H.W. Wilson Co.

Celebrations: Read-Aloud Holiday and Theme Book Program by Caroline Feller, published by the H.W. Wilson Co.

A Kick in the Head: An Everyday Guide to Poetic Forms selected by Paul B. Janeczko, Candlewick Press

TOOLS by Taro Miura, published by Chronicle Books

The Important Book by Margaret Wise Brown, published by HarperCollins

Ladybug Magazine for Ages Two to Six; Spider Magazine for ages Six to Nine:

Cricket Magazine for Ages Nine to Fourteen, published by the Cricket Magazine Group at P.O. BOX 593 in Mt. Morris, IL 61054-7666

Creating with Paper by Pauline Johnson, published by University of Washington Press

A is for airplane pilot.

Mighty Machines Airplane by Christopher Maynard, published by Dorling Kindersley

A Moon Plane by Peter McCarty, published by Henry Holt & Co.

A Day at the Airport by Richard Scarry, published by Random House Pictureback Books/Random House

Going on a Plane (Usborne First Experiences) by Anne Civardi, published by EDC Publishing

Airplane (MACHINES AT WORK) by Caroline Bingham, published by Dorling Kindersley Limited

A is for artist.

Degas and the Little Dancer: A Story about Edgar Degas by Laurence Anholt, published by Barron's

Emma by Wendy Kesselman, published by Harper & Row

The Art Lesson by Tomie dePaola, published by Paper Star/The Putnam & Grosset Group

I Ain't Gonna Paint No More! by Karen Beaumont, published by Harcourt Inc.

Visiting the Art Museum by Laurence Krasny Brown and Marc Brown, published by E.P. Dutton (reference book)

The Magical Garden of Claude Monet by Laurence Anholt, published by Barron's

Katie Meets the Impressionists by James Mayhew, published by Orchard Books

Maria Paints the Hills by Pat Mora, published by Museum of New Mexico Press

123 I Can Paint by Irene Luxbacher, published by Kids Can Press, Kids Can Press, 2250 Military Road, Tonawanda, NT 14150

Art Is Fundamental: Teaching the Elements and Principles of Art in Elementary School by Eileen S. Prince, published by Chicago Review Press

B is for baker.

An Apple Pie Tree by Zoe Hall, published by the Blue Sky Press/Imprint of Scholastic Inc.

Pumpkin Time by Zoe Hall, published by the Blue Sky Press/Imprint of Scholastic Inc.

Tony's Bread by Tomie dePaola, published by Paper Star/The Putnam & Grosset Group

Crepes by Suzette by Monica Wellington, published by Dutton Children's Books

Walter the Baker by Eric Carle, published by Scholastic Inc.

Honey Cookies by Meredith Hooker, published by Frances Lincoln Children's Books

The Apple Pie that Papa Baked by Lauren Thompson, published Simon & Schuster Books for Young Readers

Mr. Cookie Baker by Monica Wellington, published by Dutton Children's Books

Mr. Putter & Tabby Bake the Cake by Cynthia Rylant & Arthur Howard, published by Harcourt Inc.

Who Made This Cake? by Chihiro Nakagawa, published by Front Street/Boyds Mills Press, Inc.

B is for ballerina.

Time for Ballet by Adele Geras, published by Dial Books for Young Readers

Ballerina! by Peter Sis, published by Greenwillow Books/An Imprint of HarperCollins

Angelina Ballerina by Katharine Holabird, published by Pleasant Company

The Little Ballerina by Katharine Ross, published by Random House Pictureback Book/Random House

We Love Ballet! by Jane Feldman, published by Random House Pictureback Book/Random House

Ballerina Dreams by Diana White, published by Scholastic Inc.

The Story of the Nutcracker Ballet by Keborah Hautzig, published by Random House

Dream Dancer by Jill Newsome & Claudio Munoz, published by HarperCollins

Nina, Nina, Star Ballerina by Jane O'Connor, published by Grosset & Dunlap

C is for cowboy.

The Brave Cowboy by Joan Walsh Anglund, published by Andrews McMeel

Yippee - Yay! A Book about Cowboys and Cowgirls by Gail Gibbons, published by Little Brown & Co.

Cowgirl Kate and Cocoa by Erica Silverman, published by Harcourt, Inc.

Cowboy Small by Lois Lenski, published by Random House

Cowboy Camp by Tammi Sauer, published by Sterling Publishing Co., Inc.

D is for doctor.

ACHOO! Lion's Got the Flu by Hagino Chinatsu, published by Purple Bear Books

Doctor Maisy by Lucy Cousins, published by Candlewick Press

My Trip to the Hospital by Mercer Mayer, published by Harper Festival/HarperCollins

I Want to be A Doctor by Dan Liebman, published by Firefly Books

Mother Mother I Feel Sick Send for the Doctor Quick Quick Quick by Remy Charlip & Burton Supree, published by Tricycle Press

Germs! Germs! Germs! by Bobbi Katz, published by Cartwheel Books/Scholastic Inc.

From Head to Toe: The Amazing Human Body and How It Works by Barbara Seuling, published by Scholastic Inc.

Keeping You Healthy: A Book About Doctors by Ann Owen, published by Picture Window Books

D is for dentist.

My Tooth is About to Fall by Grace Maccarone, published by Scholastic, Inc.

My Wobbly Tooth Must Not Ever Never Fall Out by Lauren Child, published by Grosset & Dunlap

The Night Before the Tooth Fairy by Natasha Wing, published by Grosset & Dunlap

A Quarter from the Tooth Fairy by Caren Holtzman, published by Scholastic Inc.

Doctor DeSoto by William Steig, published by Scholastic Inc.

Just Going to the Dentist by Mercer Mayer, published by A Golden Book

Throw Your Tooth on the Roof (Tooth Traditions from Around the World) by Selby B. Beeler, published by Houghton Mifflin Co.

Albert's Toothache by Barbara Williams, published by E.P. Dutton

A Book About Your Skeleton by Ruth Belov Gross, published by Scholastic Inc.

E is for engineer.

The Little Engine That Could (Trademark) retold by Watty Piper, published by Philomel Books/Grosset & Dunlap

All Aboard ABC by Doug Magee & Robert Newman, published by Puffin Books

Freight Train by Donald Crews, published by Greenwillow books

The Train Ride by June Crebbin, published by Candlewick Press

The Little Train by Lois Lenski, published by Random House

A Train Goes Clickety-Clack by Jonathan London, published by Henry Holt & Company

Chugga-Chugga Choo-Choo by Kevin Lewis, published by Hyperion Books for Children

I Drive A Freight Train by Sarah Bridges, published by Picture Window Books

I'm Taking a Trip on My Train by Shirley Neitzel, published by Greenwillow Books

The Train to Timbuctoo by Margaret Wise Brown, published by Golden Books Co, Inc.

F is for farmer.

Old MacDonald retold by Jessica Souhami, published by Orchard Books

Our Animal Friend at Maple Hill Farm by Alice & Martin Provensen, published by Random House Books

Apples and Pumpkins by Anne Rockwell, published by MacMillan Publishing Co.

Seeds! Seeds! Seeds! by Nancy Elizabeth Wallace, published by Marshall Cavendish

The Town Mouse & the Country Mouse: An Aesop Fable adapted by Janet Stevens, published by Holiday House

Bright Barnyard by Dahlov Ipcar, published by Alfred A. Knopf

Two Little Gardeners by Margaret Wise Brown and Edith Thacher Hurd, published by A Little Golden Book Classic/Random House

Harry's Home by Catherine & Laurence Anholt, published by Farrar, Straus & Giroux

Pumpkin Town! (Or, Nothing is Better and Worse Than Pumpkins!) by Katie Mcky and Pablo Bernasconi, published by Houghton Mifflin Co.

Happy Veggies by Mayumi Oda, published by Parallax Press

The Garden in Our Yard by Greg Henry Quinn, published by Cartwheel Books/Scholastic Inc.

Town Mouse Country Mouse by Jan Brett, published by Puffin Books

Growing Vegetable Soup by Lois Ehlert, published by Scholastic Inc.

Jack's Garden by Henry Cole, published by Greenwillow Books

A Fruit is a Suitcase for Seeds by Jean Richards, published by Millbrook Press

Going to Sleep on the Farm by Wendy Cheyette Lewison, published by Dial Books for Young Readers

Big Red Barn by Margaret Wise Brown, published by HarperCollins

A Seed is Sleepy by Dianna Hutts Aston, published by Chronicle Books

F is for fireman.

Fire Truck by Peter Sis, published by Greenwillow Books

Emergency! by Gail Gibbons, published by Scholastic Inc.

Machines at Work: Fire Truck by Caroline Bingham, published by DK Publishing, Inc.

Clifford the Firehouse Dog by Norman Bridwell, published by Scholastic Inc.

The Little Fire Engine by Lois Lenski, published by Random House

Firefighter Frank by Monica Wellington, published by Puffin Books

At the Firehouse by Anne Rockwell, published by HarperCollins

G is for grocer.

General Store by Rachel Field, published by Scholastic Inc.

A Day at the Market by Sara Anderson, published by Handprint Books; 413 Sixth Avenue; Brooklyn, New York 11215

Oliver's Fruit Salad by Vivian French, published by Orchard Books

The Vegetable Alphabet Book by Jerry Pallotta and Bob Thomson, published by Charlesbridge

G is for gardener.

No More Vegetables by Nicole Rubel, published by Farrar, Straus & Giroux (See books under "F is for Farmer".)

A Seed is Sleeping by Dianna Aston, published by Chronicle Books

Tops and Bottoms adapted by Janet Stevens, published by Scholastic Inc.

Planting a Rainbow by Lois Ehlert, published by the Trumpet Club

Jack's Garden by Henry Cole, published by the Greenwillow Books

G is for garbage man.

I Stink! by Kate and Jim McMullan, published Joanna Cotler Books - An Imprint of HarperCollins Publishers

Our Garage Sale by Anne Rockwell, published by Greenwillow Books

H is for house builder.

Curious George Builds a Home adapted by Monica Perez, published by Houghton Mifflin

The Someday House by Anne Shelby, published by Orchard Books

Old MacDonald Had a Woodshop by Lisa Shulman, published by G.P. Putnam's Sons

Block City by Robert Louis Stevenson, published by E.P. Dutton

Let's Go Home by Cynthia Rylant, published by Aladdin Paperbacks,

Paper John by David Small, published by Farrar, Straus & Giroux

The Little House by Virginia Lee Burton, published by Houghton Mifflin Co.

I Want to be a Builder by Dan Liebman, published by Firefly Books

Toolbox Twins by Lola M. Schaefer, published by Henry Holt & Co.

Roxaboxen by Alice McLerran, published by Harper Collins

Tools by Taro Miura, published by Chronicle Books

H is for hairdresser.

Mop Top by Don Freeman, published by Puffin Books

Amanda's Perfect Hair by Linda Milstein, published by Tambourine Books

I is for ice cream maker.

Ice Cream: The Full Scoop by Gail Gibbons, published by Holiday House

Curious George Goes to an Ice Cream Shop edited by Margret Rey and Alan J. Shalleck, published by Houghton Mifflin Co.

J is for judge.

The Judge by Harve Zemach, published by Farrar, Straus & Giroux

What Really happened to Little Red Riding Hood: The Wolf's Story by Toby Forward, published by Candlewick Press

Clocks and More Clocks by Pat Hutchins, published by Scholastic Inc.

Nate the Great by Marjorie Sharmat, published by Coward-McCann Inc.

The Hating Book by Charlotte Zolotow, published by Harper Collins

Seven Blind Mice by Ed Young, published by Puffin Books

The Elves and the Shoemaker retold by John Cech, published by Sterling Pub

The True Story of the Three Little Pigs by Jon Scieszka, published by Puffin Books

The Tale of Peter Rabbit by Beatrix Potter, published by Grosset & Dunlap

The Hare and the Tortoise by Aesop, published by Troll Associates

Pinocchio adapted by Barbara Shook Hazen, published by Educational Reading Service, Mahwah, New Jersey

K is for kennel owner.

I Want to Be a Vet by Dan Liebman, published by Firefly Books

Animal Hospital by Judith Walker Hodge, published by DK Publishing, Inc.

Arthur's Pet Business by Marc Brown, published by Scholastic, Inc.

Moses the Kitten by James Herriot, published by St. Martin's Press

Clifford Goes to Dog School by Norman Bridwell, published by Scholastic Inc.

Dr. Dog by Babette Cole, published by Dragonfly Books

How to Be a Good Dog by Gail Page, published by Bloomsbury
    Children's Books
Pretzel by H. A. Rey, published by Houghton Mifflin Co.

L is for librarian.
    The Library by Sarah Stewart, published by Farrar, Straus & Giroux
    Wild About Books by Judy Sierra, published by Alfred A. Knopf
    Miss Smith Reads Again! by Michael Garland, published by Dutton
        Children's Book
    Book! Book! Book! by Deborah Bruss, published by Arthur A. Levine
        Books/Scholastic Inc.
    Wild About Books by Judy Sierra, published by Alfred A. Knopf
    Delilah D. at the Library by Jeanne Willis, published by Clarion
        Books
    Library Lion by Michelle Knudson and Kevin Hawkes, published
        by Candlewick Press
    Quiet! There's a Canary in the Library by Don Freeman, published
        by Golden Gate Junior Books/Scott, Foresman & Company
    Lola at the Library by Anna McQuinn, published by Scholastic Inc.

M is for mail carrier.
    My Griggs' Work by Cynthia Rylant, published by Orchard Books
    Seven Little Postmen by Margaret Wise Brown and Edith Thacher,
        published by Little Golden Books of Random House
    Flat Stanley by Jeff Brown, published by HarperCollins
    A Letter to Amy by Ezra Jack Keats, published by Viking
    Bunny Mail by Rosemary Wells, published by Viking/Penguin
        Young Readers Group
    SEND IT! by Don Carter, published by Roaring Brook Press
    The Jolly Pocket Postman by Janet & Allan Ahlberg, published
        by William Heinemann Ltd./Reed Consumer Books Ltd.
        Michelin House, 81 Fulham Road: London SW3 6RB: Great
        Britain
    Love Letters by Arnold Adoff, published by Scholastic Inc.

M is for merchant.

Caps for Sale by Esphyr Slobodkina, published by HarperCollins

On Market Street by Arnold Lobel, published by Greenwillow Books

Trucks Roll by George Ella Lyon, published by Richard Jackson Book/Atheneum Books for Young Readers

Angelita's Magic Yarn by Doris Lecher, published by Farrar, Straus & Giroux

Just Shopping with Mom by Mercer Mayer, published by Random House Pictureback Book/Random House

A Day at the Market by Sara Anderson, published by Handprint Books: 413 Sixth Avenue: Brooklyn, New York 11215

General Store by Rachel Field, published by Scholastic Inc.

Out and About at the Supermarket by Kitty Shea, published by Picture Window Books

N is for nurse.

Wash Your Hands! by Tony Ross, published by Kane/Miller Book Publishers

I Want to be a Nurse by Dan Liebman, published by Firefly Books

The Sick Day by Patricia MacLachlan, published by Dell Dragonfly Books

A Picture Book of Florence Nightingale by David A. Adler, published by Scholastic Inc.

O is for office worker.

The Old Farmer's Almanac for Kids by Yankee Publishing Inc.

Dear Deer: A Book of Homophones by Gene Barretta, published by Henry Holt and Co.

Amelia Bedelia by Peggy Parish, published by HarperCollins

Morris Has a Cold by Bernard Wiseman, published by Scholastic Inc.

Arthur Writes a Story by Marc Brown, published by Scholastic Inc.

A Chocolate Moose for Dinner by Fred Gwynne, published by Aladdin Paperbacks

A Little Pigeon Toad by Fred Gwynne, published by the Trumpet Club

Love Letters by Arnold Adoff, published by Scholastic Inc.

O is for oceanographer.

Fish Out of School by Evelyn Shaw, published by Harper & Row

Alistair Underwater by Marilyn Sadler, published by Simon & Schuster Inc.

The Octonauts & the Only Lonely Monster by Meomi, published by Immedium Inc.

Rainbow Fish and the Big Blue Whale by Marcus Pfister, published by North-South Books

Rainbow Fish Finds His Way by Marcus Pfister, published by North-South Books

Whales Passing by Eve Bunting, published by the The Blue Sky Press/Scholastic Inc.

The Magic School Bus on the Ocean Floor by Joanna Cole & Bruce Degen, published by Scholastic Inc.

A Day at the Beach by Mircea Vasiliu, published by Random House

Where the Waves Break: Life at the Edge of the Sea by Anita Malnig, published by Carolrhoda Books Inc.

Down to the Beach by May Garelick, published by Scholastic Book Services

P is for police officer.

Officer Buckle and Gloria by Peggy Rathman, published by G.P. Putnam's Sons

I Want to be a Police Officer by Dan Liebman, published by Firefly Books

Clocks and More Clocks by Pat Hutchins, published by Scholastic Inc.

Aunt Eater Loves a Mystery by Doug Cushman, published by A Harper Trophy Book/Harper & Row

The Missing Mitten Mystery by Steven Kellogg, published by Scholastic Inc.

Nate the Great by Marjorie Sharmat, published by A Yearling Book

Blueberry Shoe by Ann Dixon, published by Alaska Northwest Books

The Giant Jam Sandwich by John Vernon Lord, published by Houghton Mifflin and Co.

Too Much Noise by Ann McGovern, published by Houghton Mifflin

The Blind Men and the Elephant retold by Karen Backstein, published by Scholastic Inc.

Q is for quarterback.

What Athletes are Made of by Hanoch Piven, published by Atheneum Books for Young Readers/Simon Schuster Children's Publishing Division

Take Me Out to the Ballgame by Jack Norworth, published by Aladdin Paperbacks

Saved by the Ball by Peter Maloney and Felicia Zekauskas, published by Scholastic Inc.

Froggy Plays Soccer by Jonathan London, published by Viking

Q is for quilter.

The Quilt Story by Tony Johnston, published by Paper Star/Penguin Putnam Books for Young Readers

The Patchwork Quilt by Valerie Flournoy, published by Dial Books for Young Readers

The Quiltmaker's Gift by Jeff Brumbeau, published by Orchard Books

The Keeping Quilt by Patricia Polacco, published by Aladdin Paperbacks

Papa and the Pioneer Quilt by Jean Van Leeuwen, published by Dial Book for Young Readers

The Pumpkin Blanket by Deborah Turney Zagwyn, published by Tricycle Press

R is for rocket builder.

Curious George Gets a Medal by Margret & H. A. Rey, published by Houghton Mifflin

Alistair in Outer Space by Marilyn Sadler, published by Prentice Hall Books for Young Readers – A Division of Simon & Schuster Inc.

UFO Diary by Satoshi Kitamura, published by A Sunburst Book of Farrar, Straus & Giroux

Our Stars by Anne Rockwell, published by Scholastic Inc.

The Magic School Bus Lost in the Solar System by Joanna Cole, published by Scholastic Inc.

Comet, Stars, the Moon, and Mars: Space Poems, by Douglas Florian, published by Harcourt Inc.

Stars! Stars! Stars! by Bob Barner, published by Chronicle Books

Dogs in Space by Nancy Coffelt, published by Voyager Books/ Harcourt Brace Co.

Oxford First Book of Space by Andrew Langley, published by Oxford University Press

All Trains, Planes, and Other Things by Joan Wade Cole, published by The Economy Company

The Best Book of Spaceships by Ian Graham, published by Kingfisher, 95 Madison Avenue, New York, NY 10016

A is for Astronaut: Exploring Space from A to Z by Traci N. Todd, published by Chronicle Books

Moon Plane by Peter McCarty, published by Henry Holt and Co.

S is for singer.

Hush, Little Baby by Brian Pinkney, published by Greenwillow Books of HarperCollins

Baby Beluga by Raffi and Debi Pike, published by Crown

Wheels on the Bus (Traditional) from Raffi Songs to Read, published by Crown

Oh Where, Oh Where Has My Little Dog Gone? as told by Iza Trapani, published by Whispering Coyote Press

Down by the Station by Will Hillenbrand, published by Gulliver Books/Harcourt Brace & Co.

John Denver's Take Me Home, Country Roads adapted by Christopher Canyon, published by Dawn Pub.

The Itsy Bitsy Spider as told by Iza Trapani, published by Whispering Coyote Press

I'm a Little Teapot as told by Iza Trapani, published by Whispering Coyote Press

The Wheels on the Bus and Other Transportation Songs, published by Cartwheel Books/Scholastic Inc.

Skip to My Lou adapted by Nadine Bernard Westcott, published by Joy Street Books/Little Brown & Co.

T is for teacher.

Curious George's First Day of School by Margaret & H. A. Rey, published by Houghton Mifflin

My Teacher's Secret Life by Stephen Krensky, published by Simon & Schuster Books for Young Readers

Fred's First Day by Cathy Warren, published by Lothrop, Lee & Shepard Books

My Teacher's My Friend by P. K. Hallinan, published by Ideals Children's Books/Imprint of Hambleton-Hill Inc.

Mr. Duchy's First Day by B. G. Hennessy, published by G. P. Putnam's Sons

Miss Nelson is Missing by Harry Allard & James Marshall, published by Houghton Mifflin Co.

Timothy Goes to School by Rosemary Wells, published by Viking

David Goes to School by David Shannon, published by The Blue Sky Press/Scholastic Inc.

A Country Schoolhouse by Lynne Barasch, published by Frances Foster Books/Farrar, Straus & Giroux

Boy on the Bus by Penny Dale, published by Candlewick Press

U is for United States President

Duck for President by Doreen Cronin, published by Simon & Schuster

Arthur Meets the President by Marc Brown, published by Little, Brown & Co.

The Story of the White House by Kate Waters, published by Scholastic Inc.

House Mouse, Senate Mouse by Peter Barnes & Cheryl Shaw Barnes, published by VSP Books at P.O. Box 17011; Alexandria, VA 22302

A Picture Book of Abraham Lincoln by David A. Adler, published by The Trumpet Club

The President and Mom's Apple Pie by Michael Garland, published by Dutton Children's Books

The Buck Stops Here: The Presidents of the United States by Alice Provensen, published by The Trumpet Club

Madam President by Lane Smith, published by Hyperion Books for Children/Disney Book Group

V is for violinist.

Violet's Music by Angela Johnson, published by Dial Books for Young Readers

Mole Music by David McPhail, published by Henry Holt & Co.

Musical Max by Robert Kraus, published by Simon & Schuster Inc.

Berlioz the Bear by Jan Brett, published by The Putnam & Grosset Group

Orchestranimals by Vlasta van Kampen, published by Scholastic Inc.

Maestro Mouse and the Mystery of the Missing Baton by Peter W. Barnes and Cheryl Shaw Barnes, published by VSP Books at Books.com

Peter and the Wolf by Sergei Prokofiev, published by Alfred A. Knopf, Inc.

Animal Orchestra by Ilo Orleans, published by A Golden Book/ Random House Inc.

Fiddle-I-Fee by Will Hillenbrand, published by Gulliver Books/ Harcourt Inc.

What Instrument is This? by Rosemarie Hausherr, published by Scholastic Inc.

W is for weather reporter.

The Cloud Book by Tomie dePaola, published by Holiday House

Sun, Snow, Stars, Sky by Catherine & Laurence Anholt, published by Viking

Katy and the Big Snow by Virginia Lee Burton, published by Houghton Mifflin

Little Cloud by Eric Carle, published by Puffin Books

Cloud Boy by Rhode Montijo, published by Simon & Schuster Books for Young Readers

The Very Windy Day by Elizabeth MacDonald, published by Tambourine Books

It's Your Cloud by Joe Troiano, published by Backpack Books

Follow a Raindrop by Elsie Ward, published by Scholastic Inc.

Cloudy with a Chance of Meatballs by Judi Barrett, published Scholastic Inc.

How the Ladies Stopped the Wind by Bruce McMillan, published by Houghton Mifflin and Co.

X is for x-ray person.

A Book about your Skeleton by Ruth Belov Gross, published by Scholastic Inc.

The Skeleton Inside You by Philip Balestrino, published by Scholastic Inc.

Skeletons: An Inside Look at Animals by Jinny Johnson, published by Reader's Digest Kids

Y is for yarn maker.

A New Coat for Anna by Harriet Ziefert, published by Scholastic Inc.

No Roses for Harry! by Gene Zion, published by Scholastic Inc.

Rumpelstiltskin retold by Paul O. Zelinsky, published by E. P. Dutton

Farmer Brown Shears His Sheep by Teri Sloat, published by Dorling Kindersley Publishing Inc.

The Goat in the Rug as told to Charles L. Blood & Martin Link by Geraldine, published by Aladdin Books - Macmillan Publishing Co.

Argyle by Barbara Brooks Wallace, published by Abingdon Press

Pelle's New Suit by Elsa Beskow, published by Floris Books

Mary Was a Little Lamb by Gloria Rand, published by Henry Holt & Co.

Weaving the Rainbow by George Ella Lyon, published by Richard Jackson Book/Atheneum Books for Young Readers

One Little Lamb by Elaine Greenstein, published by Viking

Mary Had a Little Lamb by Sarah Josepha Hale, published by Scholastic Inc.

Z is for zookeeper.

Curious George Feeds the Animals by Margret & H. A. Rey, published by Houghton Mifflin Co.

Animalia by Graeme Base, published by Harry N. Abrams, Inc.

The Zoo by Suzy Lee, published by Kane/Miller Book Publishers

Animal Strike at the Zoo: It's True! by Karma Wilson, published by HarperCollins

The Great Zoo Hunt! by Pippa Unwin, published by Doubleday

The Zoo Room by Louise Schofield, published by Simply Read Books

I Want to be a Zookeeper by Dan Liebman, published by Firefly Books

1, 2, 3 to the Zoo: A Counting Book by Eric Carle, published by Philomel Books

I Had a Cat by Mona Rabun Reeves, published by Aladdin Paperbacks

An Egg is Quiet by Dianna Hutts Aston, published by Chronicle Books

The Doctor in the Zoo by Dr. Lester E. Fisher, published by Rand McNally & Co.

Printed in the United States
By Bookmasters